BASIC ENGLISH GRAMMAR AND USAGE
FOR TERTIARY INSTITUTIONS

Ubong E. Josiah (PhD)
Aaron N. Nwoke (M.A.)

Basic English Grammar and Usage

Ubong E. Josiah (Ph.D)
Aaron N. Nwoke (M.A.)

JUBE-EVANS Books and Publications
SW 718 Down Hospital Road
Near Sauki Clinic
P.O.Box 845
Bida, Niger State
Nigeria

All rights reserved. No reproduction, copy or transmission of this publication may be made in any form or by any means, electronic or electrical, including photocopying, recording or otherwise without the prior written permission of the publishers.

First printed   2009
First published   2009
Revised edition   2015
Second revision   2017

JUBE-EVANS Books and Publications
ISBN 978-978-48934-0-4

ACKNOWLEDGEMENTS

This book is an outcome of the efforts of many scholars, colleagues, friends and our students in tertiary institutions of learning. First, we want to thank our numerous students, first, at The Federal Polytechnic, Bida, Niger State, and secondly, at the University of Uyo, who were our greatest source of inspiration in producing this book in the form it is. Some of the poor performances of our students, rather than deter us, became the source of encouragement and inspiration, which spurred us into the writing of this book on grammar. Added to this, some of the students actually demanded that a comprehensive book which can address some seemingly difficult aspects of grammar and usage problems be written so as to proffer remedial solutions to the common grammatical errors noticed in their written, and possibly, spoken grammar. We ultimately yielded to the pressures mounted by those students, and the outcome is this text on grammar and usage. We are most grateful to our numerous students in this respect.

Dr. Sunday Ogala and Dr. Audu Tonga were amiable colleagues whose contributions to this book are worth mentioning. They were very meticulous in proofreading the manuscript to the extent that even seemingly infinitesimal errors, particularly, those dealing with mechanics were pointed out to the authors. We quite appreciate their efforts.

We also want to show appreciation to Professor J. S. Aliyu of Ahmadu Bello University (ABU), Zaria; Professor Sola T. Babatunde of the University of Ilorin, Ilorin; Professor David Eka and Dr. Juliet Udoudom of the University of Uyo, Uyo, who made very useful contributions by providing the fundamental and basic insights that led to the writing of this text. We pray that God will reward them abundantly.

Dr. Romanus Aboh and Dr. Maria-Helen Eka, both of the Department of English, University of Uyo, had also been instrumental to shaping the contents of the text. Their pains-taking, proofreading, remarks and suggestions helped in shaping the current version of the text. We are most grateful.

We also wish to thank our wives and children for their understanding and support which they show to us while the writing of this book lasted. We pray that the good Lord will reward them for their patience, endurance and prayers.

Finally, we use this medium to reverence the Almighty God Who gave us sound health, wisdom, knowledge and understanding that enabled us to put together the information contained in this book.

Indeed, we are grateful to all.

Basic English Grammar and Usage

DEDICATION

*Dedicated to the Almighty God;
and, our wives and children.*

PREFACE

At a time when the performance of students in tertiary institutions is becoming abysmally poor and embarrassing, the need to provide standard textbooks on grammar that can bridge the gap created by obvious lack of adequate and standardized textbooks as well as qualified teachers of grammar in many institutions of higher learning becomes inevitable. This informs the situation that necessitated the writing of ***Basic English Grammar and Usage.*** As the title clearly indicates, the book is intended to expose readers to both the basic elements of the English grammar, and then, address usage problems usually associated with the poor knowledge of learners and users of the English language.

As a starting point, the book x-rays the origin of the English language with a view to pointing out why the language generally behaves the way it does – it is an outcome of several languages of the world (Anglo-Saxon, Latin, Greek, French and other Indo-European, and specifically, West Germanic languages, among others), and as such manifests several orthographic and phonological patterns, sometimes seemingly illogical in nature, as well as divergent grammatical models, varying word structure, and so on as outcomes of the influence of these foreign languages that streamed into the English language. Equally, that the language is analytic in nature is meticulously examined and explicated.

Particularly, the chapter on spelling attempts to isolate distinctly, some prominent, exoglossic standards by which acceptable English vocabulary and grammar could be measured, British or American. In this section, too, some rules of spellings are generally theorized to give vent to memory. Chapters Three, Four and Five specifically handle different aspects of English mechanics namely punctuation, capitalization of letters and paragraph. These chapters are considered as vital pre-requisites to appropriate writing skills for English learners.

Chapter Six deals with the delicate aspect of the English orthography and pronunciation, specifically, homophones. Here, English homophones are elaborately treated, not just to point out the difficulties that English learners encounter in grappling with the seemingly illogical orthography and spelling of some English words, but also to provide clues to the confusion experienced in pronouncing such words. The unique handling of this section proves that with careful study, the problem can be overcome.

Chapter Seven is on the parts of speech in English. This section sets out to establish the basic foundation for beginners in advanced level of English grammar relating to English *form classes*. It conventionally treats the eight parts of speech for which English is known to have, and then, elaborates on several sub-divisions of English *form classes*. Both lexical and inflectional forms of the word classes are elaborately highlighted.

Chapter Eight deals with English morphological forms. In this section, English word structure is meticulously examined so as to provide essential insight into English lexis and structure, and generally, English vocabulary. Lexical morphology, which deals with word formation processes as well as inflectional morphology, which treats grammatical properties are explored and given in-depth treatment.

Phrases, clauses and sentence structures are considered next in the series making the contents of Chapters Nine, Ten and Eleven respectively. These three sections are handled discretely since they form the core concept of the grammar of English. It is necessary to point out that since this is just a basic grammar book, notions relating to generative grammar and other more advanced models of grammar are not handled here. Such aspects will be treated in another volume.

Chapter Twelve is on Vocabulary Development and is treated as an aspect that provides in-road to acquiring a repository of English words for everyday use in communicating exactly what one has in mind. This chapter concentrates mostly on English synonyms and antonyms as a way of making available adequate vocabularies for English users to explore for semantic explicitness.

The section on Concord forms the last chapter of this book. This chapter, making the thirteenth chapter, is aimed at explicating the tenuous concept of cohesiveness, collocations and grammatical harmony in written English composition. It discusses different aspects of grammatical relations between subject and verb, pronoun and their antecedents and other forms of grammatical harmony.

The section on glossary is an appendage that supplies the clues to understanding the various grammatical and linguistic concepts used throughout the text. It is hoped that readers will find this section very useful since it provides basic conceptual clarifications to the contents of the entire text.

Generally, the book is written in simple, down-to-earth, interpretable language, and we do hope that readers will find the materials presented in this text very useful in understanding the basic grammar of the English language.

TABLE OF CONTENTS

Acknowledgements	iv
Dedication	v
Preface	vi
Table of Contents	ix
Chapter One: A Short History of the English Language	1
Definition of Language	1
Origin of the English Language	4
The English Language: Phases of Development	5
Old English	5
Middle English	8
Modern English	10
Chapter Two: Spellings	14
Introduction to English Spellings	14
Spellings in British and American English	15
Spellings Influenced by Parts of Speech	25
Difficult Spellings	35
Spellings Influenced by Irregular and Confusing Plural Forms	39
Spellings Influenced by Irregular Tense forms	49
Spelling of Diminutives	52
Chapter Three: Punctuation	55
The Full Stop or Period	56
The Comma	58
The Semi-colon	61
The Colon	63
The Question Mark	64
The Exclamation Mark	65
The Dash	66
Parenthesis or Brackets	67
The Quotation Marks or Inverted Commas	68
The Hyphen	69
The Apostrophe	70
The Ellipsis	71

The Tilde	72
The Virgule	72
The Caret	72
The Asterisk	73
The Braces	73
Chapter Four: Capitalization of Letters	**74**
Uses of Capital Letters	74
Capitalization of Homonyms	77
Chapter Five: The Paragraph	**80**
Meaning and Function of Paragraph	80
The Topic Sentence	80
The Qualities of a Good Paragraph	81
Methods of Paragraph Development	84
Types of Paragraph	86
Length of the Paragraph	88
Special Purpose Paragraph	88
Pitfalls to Avoid in the Development of the Paragraph	94
Chapter Six: Homophones and Other Confusing Words	**99**
Chapter Seven: Parts of Speech	**125**
Classification of Parts of Speech	125
Open-System Group	125
Closed-System Group	126
Description of the Parts of Speech	127
Noun	127
Pronoun	131
Verb	134
Tense	135
Aspect of the Verb	144
Adjectives	146
Adverb	148
Preposition	149
Conjunction	151
Interjections	151
Chapter Eight: The English Word Structure	**153**

Morphology: Its Meaning and Content	153
Inflectional Morphology	154
Variations in English Inflectional Morphemes	155
Lexical Morphology	159
Patterns of English Lexical Morphemes	159
Affixation	160
Prefixation	161
Infixation	161
Suffixation	163
Compounding	165
Blends	166
Back-formations	166
Reduplication	167
Conversion	167
Chapter Nine: Phrases	169
Types of Phrases	170
Noun Phrase	170
Verb Phrase	173
Adjectival Phrase	176
Adverbial Phrase	179
Prepositional Phrase	181
Chapter Ten: Clauses	182
Types of Clauses	182
Types of Subordinate Clause	185
Noun Clause	185
Adjectival or Relative Clause	187
Adverbial Clause	189
Types of Adverbial Clause	190
Chapter Eleven: The Sentence	194
Classification of Sentences	195
Functional Sentences	195
Structural Sentences	197
The Sentence Structure	201
Sentence Elements	202

Voice and Mood in Sentences   209

Chapter Twelve: Vocabulary Development   214
Introduction   214
Synonyms and Antonyms   215
Synonyms   215
Antonyms   225
Chapter Thirteen: Concord   229
Concord of Number between Subject and Verb   229
Pronoun/ Antecedent Concord   237
Shifts in Construction   243
Chapter Sixteen: A Glossary of Grammatical and Linguistic Terms   250
References   264

CHAPTER ONE

A SHORT HISTORY OF THE ENGLISH LANGUAGE

1.1 Introductory Background

In this first chapter, a brief insight into the general definition of language is essential in order to highlight the discussion on the history of the English language. The intention is obvious: to provide the preliminary purview within which the discussion in this book will be anchored. There are many definitions of language put forward by various authors. We will not spend time discussing many individual definitions since that does not form a major part of our pre-occupation in this text. Rather, our interest will be to examine just a few of the definitions of language and then make some general remarks.

One of the definitions of language by Essien (2003) cited in Essien (2006, p.2), in what appears to be a review of several definitions of language (from Sapir, 1921 to Chomsky, 1968 to Cameron, 1990 and Essien, 1990), is that:

> Language is a system of structured vocal symbols by means of which human beings make meaning and communicate and interact with each other in a given community. Put more simply, language is a system of rules and principles to which sound, structure and meaning are integrated for communication.

Another definition by Osisanwo (2003) cited in Osisanwo (2008, p.2) sees language as "human vocal noise or the graphic representation of this noise used systematically and conventionally by members of a speech community for purposes of communication". In the view of Gimson and Cruttendon (1994), language is a system of conventional signals used for communication by a whole community. This source adds that such pattern of conventions covers a system of significant sound units (phonemes), the inflection and arrangement of words and the association of meaning with words.

Rice-Johnson's (2008) proposal presented in the following excerpt subtly introduces the concept of logic into the definition of the human language. The definition states that:

> Language is the process or set of processes used to ensure there is agreement between the sender and receiver for meanings assigned to the symbols and the schema for combining them used for each communication.

Here, language is conceived of in terms of 'a process' or 'a set of processes' that makes use of consciously systematized categories of arbitrary phonic symbols in the form of a schema (symbols, which in themselves are not meaningful or logical) to facilitate communication between *interactants* or interlocutors living within the ambience of a linguistically identifiable culture. By inference, William Rice-Johnston (himself a Mathematician) cleverly explores the logical content of the human language, although that is not explicitly stated, but the words 'process' and 'schema' are exponents of this notion.

One typical deduction from these definitions is the fact that language is a rule–governed human behaviour, primarily phonic and arbitrary in nature, with those phonic materials generally structured by convention in a way capable of facilitating communication and human interaction within a definable linguistic community. Another apparent inference we can draw from these definitions is that language is peculiarly a human trait, generally located within the human society and, as it were, adapts itself to the norms and values of the society within which it is situated (cf Jowitt, 1991; Banjo, 1996; Brann, 2006). This implies that the human language ultimately derives its intelligibility from the society where it exists or from the situation of context within which it occurs and is characterised by its inelastic variability, limitless versatility and interminable, plural complexity (Josiah, 2014).

A synthesis of the defintions of language we have treated so far is this: any non-instinctive and acceptable system of human communication which employs arbitrary vocal sounds and graphic symbols as well as non-vocal signs and signals in the expression of thoughts, feelings, ideas or concepts within specific speech communities (see Josiah, 1994). However, in this text, we would re-define language as both an illogical and a rational human behavior thus:

> a plurality of complex sets of arbitrary vocal symbols, visual signs and aural-oral signals, which are adapted by convention and functionally structured logically for purposes of communication and interaction within geographically defineable linguistic communities (see Josiah, 2009).

Two major inferences can be gleaned from all the definitions presented by language experts all through the ages: that language is primarily speech and, therefore, basically phonic in nature while the orthographic form is merely a way of documenting that speech; and that language is both a logical and an arbitrary human behaviour.

From the remarks made up to this point, we will treat the English language, like every other natural language, both as a spoken and a written language, with the spoken form having existed from inception, and the written form assuming its orthographic form much later, mostly by about the 15th century A.D. after the invention of the printing press by William Caxton. At present, the English language, has attained the status of a global language and is one of the most widely-spoken language the world over. These remarks form the background of our discussion on the historical outlay of the English language in particular, and the general grammar of the language in general.

1.2 Origin of the English Language

It is important to indicate here that the purpose of this section is not only to enlighten the reader on the history of the English language but also to show the evolutionary trends of the basic English mechanics and grammar which occurred through the different phases as the language developed from an arbitrary, oral form and an illogical, orthographic pattern to a system that has become linguistically standardized.

Every human language has a trace of its original or "ancestral" home and a course of historical development through time. English language exhibits these characteristics from its inception. The word "English" was first used by Wessex King, Alfred the Great (871-899 A.D.) and Abbot Aelfric to refer to the general language of England, p.1 During that time, the two letters "sc" were pronounced /ʃ/, as in "sh", so the language was written 'Englisc' instead of English.

Originally, English language belongs to an ancestral language family called Indo-European (Baugh, 1976, Pp.22-23). The expression "Indo-European" refers to a set of linguistic forms which embody the language of a greater part of the present-day Europe, Iran and India[2]. It can equally be referred to as Indo-Germanic or Aryan family of languages which existed by about 3000 B.C. Of course, the Indo-European language was primarily an unwritten language.

There are generally nine major subdivisions of the Indo-European languages. One of these major subdivisions is the Germanic group to which English language ultimately belongs. More specifically, English language is a branch of the Low Germanic group of languages. In its earliest form, the language was known as Old English (O.E.) or Anglo-Saxon. This version of

English was spoken by a group of Germanic invaders namely Angles, Saxons and Jutes (cf Jowitt, 2009).

In practice, the etymology (that is, the history of the origin of words or word roots) of English vocabulary shows a variety of large number of word-borrowing and coinage from other Indo-European languages in particular, and other languages of the world in general. This is noticeable in the spelling and structure of English words.

1.3   The English Language: Phases of Its Development

In discussing its course of development, English language can be arbitrarily divided into three major phases namely: Old English (450 – 1100 A.D.); Middle English (1100 – 1500 A.D.); and Modern English (1500 A.D. to the present day).

1.3.1   Old English (OE)

The exact period for the inception of the Old English cannot be ascertained. Nevertheless, the language evolved from the incursions of a group of three closely-related Germanic tribes – the Angles, the Saxons and the Jutes – who invaded England by the middle of the 5th century A.D. This invasion brought large changes into and almost replaced the original language of the Britons, which was Celtic. Following that invasion, OE became a constitution of four main dialects namely West-Saxon, Kentish, Northumbrian and Mercian.

However, the West Saxon dialect exerted more influence on OE than the others mainly because of the political situation that favoured it at the time. For instance, Wessex had political dominance over various Anglo-Saxon kingdoms (Baugh, 1976). Thus, the West-Saxon dialect provided the earliest recorded document of the English language.

During this period of the English language, some letters, which are not familiar to the present-day English scholars, were used. According to Brook (1958, p.43), "many of the letters used in OE manuscripts differ in shape from their modern equivalents.' For example, OE used some letter forms and sounds which, if compared to the present-day letters, seem strange. Here are some examples of such letters.

ð   for th (voiced)
ʃ   for s
þ   for w or th (voiceless)
ŕ   for r
æ   for a or e (æsc) pronounced ash.
c   for k
sc   for sh

OE equally used some scribal contractions to represent certain words e.g '7' for 'and'.[3]

Relatively, the OE that was written down in manuscripts appeared as if it were "continuous prose, without caesura markings, without line divisions, without punctuation, except the full-stop" (Kermode et al 1973, p.19). Such include the specimens of OE poetry such as "Caedmon's Hymn", "Beowulf", "Dream of the Rood", "The Battle of Maldon", Bede's *Ecclesiastical History of the English People* and OE translation of the "The Lord's Prayer". In essence, punctuation marks were rarely used at this stage of English writing.

Equally, Old English words were different in form and in spelling from modern English words. Compare the following words.

OE	ME	OE	ME
stan	stone	rune	run
gan	go	ostre	oyster
cene	keen	faran	travel
fyr	fire	preo	three
hlud	loud	feo	fee
heafod	head	hu	how
hlaf	loaf	scip	sheer
ban	bone	bæc	back

modor	mother	heah	high
sunne	sun	bæð	bath
ozan	own	sawol	soul

Note that these OE words are now obsolete in modern English. The patterns of OE sentences were apparently different from those of modern English in terms of content and structure. Examine the following examples:

Old English: Thu eart god mon.
Modern English: You are a good man.
Old English: God blets-O-de Noe and his sun-a and cwoeth hem to weax-ath and be-oth gemenigfil-de and a-fyll-ath th-a eort-an.
Modern English: God blessed Noah and his sons, and said unto them, "be fruitful and multiply and replenish the earth" (Gen. 9, p.1).

From the examples given here, one notices the differences that have occurred between Old and Modern English. As a consequence, a great deal of Old English words have contributed immensely to the basic vocabulary and grammar of the present-day English.

However, certain historical events brought remarkable changes into OE. One of such events was the christianising of Britain in 597 A.D. by St. Augustine. This event brought English into liberal contact with Latin civilization and registered significant additions to the vocabulary of OE.

Again, in the 8th and 9th century A.D., OE manifested further changes following the Scandinavian invasion basically caused by the Vikings from Norway and Denmark. This brought about considerable mixture of the races and their languages with OE.

A third event was the Norman invasion and subsequent conquest of England in 1066 A.D after the Battle of Hastings. This brought into English, a large number of French loan-words. After this invasion, French became the language of government, literature, law, religion and administration amidst Latin and Greek vocabularies earlier introduced into the language. This explains why there are many French words today in the English language. Of course, because of the influence of Norman French on the English soil at that time, a resultant dialect known as Anglo-Norman emerged.

Many of the words that came into English during these invasions culminated in the emergence of words that were to form the synonyms of the English language at a later stage of development. Again, these invasions ultimately served to trigger-off a new phase of English between A.D. 1100 and 1500 which is arbitrarily coined the "Middle English" (ME).

1.3.2 Middle English (ME)

Certain factors aided the development of the Middle English. London was the nerve centre of the nation. It was the melting-pot for social interaction, political activities, cultural development, and linguistic studies. Also, the period witnessed the revival of abandoned national values. Scholars with diverse economic interests, political leanings, religious inclinations linguistic appetite and cultural flavour emerged. Such scholars include Geoffrey Chaucer, John Gower and later, King James, William Shakespeare, Samuel Johnson and Noah Webster. These scholars, who were products of unique intellectual centres like Oxford and Cambridge Universities, wrote various literatures in English using the East Midland dialect which had gained distinctive currency at the time more than the other dialects in the Middle English period.

Moreover, the devastating epidemic called the "Black Death" and the victory gained in the Hundred Years' war of the

15th century brought about a consensus national interest which resulted in cultural development, the growth of nationalism and national commitment. This growing national unity promoted the growth of the English language as a lingua franca. By this time, however, English had become a mixture of French, Latin, Old English, Greek, German – to mention just a few.

Most of all, the changes that occurred in the ME was climaxed in the 15th century with the introduction of the wooden printing press by William Caxton at Westminster in 1476 A.D. The art of printing was instrumental to the development of standard orthography for the English language. With the introduction of the printing press, English spellings became standardized and with this came the documentation of cultural, religious and administrative records. In fact, some of the spellings used by Caxton's men (who were Dutch), although illogical, are still being used in English language today. For instance, the guttural 'gh' was used to represent "f" (as in enough, tough, and so on). All these account for the awkward and illogical spellings we have in English language today.

Furthermore, during the Middle English period, Latin, French and Greek were the dominant languages used. Latin was very prominent because it was the language of education, religion and science. Many books were written in Latin. Several church activities were also conducted in Latin.

Relatively, the ME period was the time when the learning of English was resurrected and the conservative barriers to the development of the language were gradually removed by the rulers. It should be noted, however, that it was through the rural folk that English was preserved during the reign of French Normans in England. Moreover, the loss of Normandy by King John in 1204 resulted in a speedy resurrection of English in England (cf Brook, 1958).

The major changes that brought about differences between OE and ME include the following. First, there was extensive 'levelling' or general removal of inflectional endings which was prominent during the OE period. For example, words like blets-o-de became blessed; be-oth became be, sunne became son, and so on, as indicated earlier. Second, there was strict adherence to normal word-order in the language. In essence, the language (formerly synthetic in nature) gradually became analytic (i.e. relatively uninflected). Thirdly, the ME period witnessed the introduction of large number of French loan-words and widespread modification of English spellings to achieve uniformity between English and French spellings. Finally, although there was no unified orthography at this time, final unaccented vowels became completely eliminated in English words and this affected the nouns and verbs. With these changes, other remarkable features emerged to drag down another phase in the development of English as a language. This phase is known as the Modern English period.

1.3.3 Modern English

Some historical prologues gingered the development of Modern English (MOE) which manifested some distinctive features at about the beginning of 1500 A.D. Such historical harbingers were not unconnected with the frenzied epoch of scientific and geographical discoveries of the age.

First, the introduction of the art of printing was a major boost to the development of authentic and conventional orthography of English. In addition, Christopher Columbus' discovery of the West Indies ultimately led to the discovery of America. Again, Vasco Da Gama (a Portuguese Sailor) wrote a great Navigation Myth around 1490 A.D after he rounded up the Cape of Good Hope. Finally, the first dictionary of English language written by Samuel Johnson in 1755 A.D. greatly helped to stabilize English orthography. All these developments brought about massive enlargement of the English vocabulary because of its wide contact with other parts the world (see Baugh, 1976).

Also, these events relatively created a conducive atmosphere for learning and research into various fields and consequently enhanced the development of the vocabulary of the English language.

Of course, the Renaissance Movement, which occurred at the time, brought about the revival of culture and an insatiable quest for knowledge. The result was the establishment of institutions of learning and the production of many literatures written in English. During the time, Greek was considered the language of excellence and was studied in English universities. Thus, Greek had influence on the English language as a result of its use as the language of instruction.

Finally, the Reformation Movement which started about that time had great impact on the English culture. Spearheaded by Martin Luther from Germany and Zwingli from Switzerland, the movement emphasized that the mother tongue should be used to preach the word of God to the people. As a result of this movement, the leaders questioned the rationale behind some of the practices of the Roman Catholic Church. Consequently, there was a break away from the influence of Roman Catholicism and that meant a major set-back to the use of Latin which was mostly employed by Roman Catholic Church for religious venerations. All these events virtually helped in widening the fringes of the English vocabulary and, ultimately, its grammar.

The major characteristics that featured during this phase of English include the following:

a) There was a large number of borrowed words from a variety of sources such as Greek, Latin, German, Russian, Spanish, Italian, French, and so on.
b) The discoveries of Christopher Columbus and Vasco Da Gama brought about the introduction of new names for things discovered. At the same time, Spanish, West Indian

and African words were injected into English and these helped to enrich the vocabulary of the language.
c) The language became entirely analytic. Analytic language is one that makes extensive use of prepositions and auxiliary verbs and depends upon strict word order to show other relationships (cf Essien, 1990). In this sense, final syllabic sounds which were present in Middle English were either entirely removed or retained to give length to the preceding vowel.

Besides, the Modern English period occurred in four different phases namely:
    i. The period between 1500 and 1625 which marked the death of King James;
    ii. The period between 1650 and 1699 after the death of John Dryden;
    iii. The period between 1700 to about 1930; and
    iv. The period between 1930 to the present day.

In each of these periods, several changes were recorded both in pronunciation and grammar of Modern English. This explains the observable differences that are noticeable between Elizabethan or Shakespearean English and that of the present-day English.

Finally, a review of the discussions in this section shows that many changes have occurred in the English language since its inception. Many words have been borrowed into the language by way of conquest, contact and coinage to boost the vocabulary of the language. Thus, the awkward or illogical spelling forms, the variant punctuation marks, the divergent grammatical structures as well as the synonyms and antonyms of English which pose problems to English users today are traceable to the extensive borrowing capacity of the English language from many languages of the world that have helped to enrich its grammar for many centuries now.

NOTES TO CHAPTER ONE
1. See William Benton, "English Language." *Encyclopaedia Britanica* (1945), VI, Pp. 879.
2. See William Benton, "English Language." *Encyclopaedia Britanica* (1945), VI, Pp. 874
3. See Frank Kermode et al, 'Caedmon's Hymn," *Oxford Anthology of English Literature* (1973), I, Pp. 19.

CHAPTER TWO

SPELLINGS

One major consideration in observing mechanical accuracy in any written discourse is the use of correct spellings in documenting the orthographic form of the language. In this chapter, therefore, English spellings will be examined from various perspectives in order to expose the reader to the various confusing spelling forms which occur in English language. We will informally try to formulate arbitrary principles that could aid memory and so be of help to English learners during writing.

An Introduction to English Spellings

Generally, English spellings cannot be formulated into pontificated set of rules. This is because they are largely and invariably illogical in form and confusing in practice. By extension, the illogical nature of English spellings can be traced to the large scale "streams of words" borrowed from various languages of the world into the language. This largely explains why there are various spelling patterns in the English language today. Relatively, the system of English orthography does not absolutely reflect the pronunciation of words.

Besides, the meagre twenty-six letters of alphabet in the language are grossly inadequate to provide sufficient, independent letters for more unique spelling forms than it obtains in the language presently. Therefore, to achieve a more definite morphological structure, some letters are employed repeatedly and consistently to enhance word-formation processes in an inexhaustible way. However, this cannot be accomplished without recurrent complications. This is why the study of English spellings is not only indispensable to scholars, but also an activity that requires utmost concentration and relentless practice.

Some major variations occur in the spellings of words in both British and American English. This is attributed to cultural and environmental influences as well as the activities of lexicographers. Thus, a great deal of varying differences occur, not only in the oral forms of both British and American English, but also in the written forms as well. One key remark to make here is that British spelling mostly uses –ise in words like analyse, realise, bastardise, whereas American English mostly adopts –ize in the same position. There are a large number of other variant forms as could be seen below. Examine the following examples.

BE	AME	BE	AME
all right	alright	ampoule	ampule
analyse	analyze	borsch	borscht
Benedick	Benedict	catalogue	catalog
candour	candor	centre	center
cigarette	cigaret	colour	color
defence	defense	distil	distill
disyllabic	dissyllabic	draught	draft
enamour	enamor	epilogue	epilogue
faeces	feces	flavour	flavor
favour	favor	foetus	fetus
fervour	fervor	fogey	fogy
forbear	forebear	fulfil	fulfill
furore	furor	gramme	gram
gibe	jibe	groyne	groin
gruelling	grueling	guage	gage
instil	instill	intern	interne
jewellery	jewelry	liquorice	licorice
labour	labor	litre	liter
licence	license	louvre	louver
lustre	luster	mat or matt	matte
manilla	manila	manoeuvre	maneuver
mattins	matins	meagre	meager

15

metre	meter	mitre	miter
mould	mold	moult	molt
moustache	mustache	nitre	niter
ochre	ocher	offence	offense
odour	odor	parlour	parlor
pyjamas	pajamas	pedagogue	pedagog
petrol	gasoline (gas)	piastre	piaster
philtre	philter	pretence	pretense
practise (v)	practice (v)	programme	program
practice (n)	practise (n)	reconnoitre	reconnoiter
rancour	rancor	rhyme	rime
realise	realize	rumour	rumor
sabre	saber	salt-petre	salt-peter
sanatorium	sanatarium	saviour	savior
savour	savor	savoury	savory
scallywag	scalawag	sceptic	skeptic
sceptre	scepter	sillabub	syllabub
skilful	skillful	slew	slue
slug	slog	smoulder	smolder
staunch	stanch	storey	story (building)
succour	succor	sulpha	sulfa
sulphate	sulfate	sulphide	sulfide
sulphur	sulfur	tumour	tumor
theatre	theater	tyre	tire
unsavoury	unsavoury	vapour	vapor
valour	valor	vice	vise
vigour	vigor	wilful	wilful
waggon	wagon	woollen	woollen

Varying spellings also occur in the past tense forms of both Englishes as illustrated below:

BRITISH ENGLISH	AMERICAN ENGLISH
jewelled	jeweled
travelled	traveled
crenellated	crenelated
cancelled	canceled
unrivalled	unrivaled
parcelled	parceled
dishevelled	disheveled

Note: The following spelling rules can be deduced from the spellings of both American and British English highlighted so far.

a) Some words ending with "-our" in British English take only "-or" for the American English, e.g.:

BRITISH ENGLISH	AMERICAN ENGLISH
candour	candor
colour	color
flavour	flavor
fervour	fervor
favour	favor
labour	labor.

b) Some words ending with "-gue: in British English stop with only "-g" in American equivalent, e.g.:

BRITISH ENGLISH	AMERICAN ENGLISH
catalogue	catalog
dialogue	dialog
epilogue	epilog
pedagogue	pedagog.

c) Some words having "-re" ending in British English take "-er" ending in American version.

BRITISH ENGLISH	AMERICAN ENGLISH
calibre	caliber
centre	center
litre	liter
meagre	meager
metre	meter
sceptre	scepter.

d) Few words ending with a single "-l" in British English take "-ll" in final position for the American English, e.g.:

BRITISH ENGLISH	AMERICAN ENGLISH
distil	distill
fulfil	fulfill
instil	instill

e) Some words with "-ce" ending in British English take "-se" ending in American equivalent, e.g.:

BRITISH ENGLISH	AMERICAN ENGLISH
defence	defense
licence	license
offence	offense
pretence	pretense

f) It is equally important to note that whereas British English sometimes exhibit consonant doubling within words, the American English equivalent does not exhibit such characteristics in some cases. See some examples below:

BRITISH ENGLISH	AMERICAN ENGLISH
manilla	manila
woollen	woolen
gruelling	grueling
mattins	matins
programme	program

British English	American English
jewellery	jewelry
scallywag	scalawag
waggon	wagon

However, there are exceptions to this pattern as follows:

BRITISH ENGLISH	AMERICAN ENGLISH
skilful	skillful
wilful	wilful

g) Again, while British maintain "-y" in medial positions in some words, Americn English uses "-i" instead, e.g.:

BRITISH ENGLISH	AMERICAN ENGLISH
groyne	groin
rhyme	rime
tyre	tire

h) British spelling sometimes uses –"ph" as opposed to "-f" used by the American English equivalent, e.g.:

BRITISH ENGLISH	AMERICAN ENGLISH
sulpha	sulfa
sulphate	sulfate
sulphide	sulfide
sulphur	sulphur

i) There are some words in British and American English which are equally distinct in spelling without a uniform pattern. Here are few examples of such words:

BRITISH ENGLISH	AMERICAN ENGLISH
realize	realise
vice	vise
analyse	analyze

It should be noted, however, that English Language, like other languages of the world, is arbitrary in nature. It, therefore, becomes difficult to theorise its spelling or to provide a more general rule for the spelling of words, either in American or British English. Moreso, both American and British English conventionally use some words commonly without any change in spellings. For instance, both American and British English use words like nacre, massacre, padre, mediocre, cadre, monologue, prologue, prorogue and many other without any change in spelling.

j) Many English words with final "-ze" or "-se" neither indicate American spelling nor British spelling. Rather, most of such words are variant forms for the same word which can be used interchangeably whether in British English or American English. However, it has been observed that British spelling mostly uses *-ise*, while *-ize* is also used but sparingly, mainly in publications of the Oxford University Press and particularly by the *Oxford English Dictionary* (see comments inWikipaedia online Dictionary). But the American spelling makes use of the –ize spellings while –ise is carefully avoided. Various examples of such words are listed below.

anglicize	-	anglicise
authorize	-	authorise
baptize	-	baptise
bastardize	-	bastardise
categorize	-	categorise
democratize	-	democratise
emphasize	-	emphasise
equalize	-	equalise
familiarize	-	familiarise
finalize	-	finalise
galvanize	-	galvanise
generalize	-	generalise
harmonize	-	harmonise
hospitalize	-	hospitalise

idealize	-	idealise
immortalize	-	immortalise
jeopardize	-	jeopardise
legalize	-	legalise
localize	-	localise
memorize	-	memorise
mobilize	-	mobilise
nationalize	-	nationalise
naturalize	-	naturalise
organize	-	organise
oxidize	-	oxidise
penalize	-	penalise
politicize	-	politicise
rationalize	-	rationalise
recognize	-	recognise
scrutinize	-	scrutinise
symbolize	-	symbolise
theorize	-	theorise
trivialize	-	trivialise
urbanize	-	urbanise
utilize	-	utilise
visualize	-	visualise
vulcanize	-	vulcanise
westernize	-	westernise
womanize	-	womanise

Caution is necessary in the use of these variants forms. First, there is a strong modern trend by various schools of thought to either maintain consistency in the spelling of words or to use the two spellings with equal intensity. Second, it should be noted that although these words are variant forms, the British English conventionally uses the variant form ending with "-ize" more than the "-ise" ending while American spelling conventionally adopts the "ise" ending more than the "-ize" variant. But, virtually and arbitrarily, both American and British English use both spellings interchangeably.

    Again, it is more ideal for speakers or users of British English to be consistent in using the "-ize" endings in formal writing. However, whichever variant form one chooses to use, there should be consistency. Generlly, students are advised to use the "-ize" form in writing British oriented English. Moreso, it is worthy to note that some words in British English originally have the final "-ize" or '-ise' as the case may be without any alternative as seen in the words below:

    surprise
    comprise
    revise
    advise
    advertise
    exercise
    supervise
    size
    prize.

k)   In addition to the variation in spellings stated above, there are other variant forms which could be used interchangeably particularly in British English. Below are a list of words with such spelling forms:

aesthetic	-	esthetic
amok	-	amuck
archaeology	-	archeology
artifact	-	artefact
ascendancy	-	ascendancy
autogiro	-	autogyro
ax	-	axe
balk	-	bulk
bandoleer	-	bandolier
banian	-	banyan

bannister	-	banister
bortsch	-	borsch
by-law	-	bye-law
caldron	-	cauldron
caliph	-	calif
carcass	-	carcase
chantey	-	chanty, shantey
chile	-	chilli, chille
cicatrice	-	cicatrix
connection	-	connexion
crosier	-	crozier
curtsey	-	curtsy
daemon	-	demon
dietician	-	dietician
disk	-	disc
dispatch	-	despatch
dyke	-	dike
empale	-	impale
enrole	-	enrol
enrolment	-	enrollment
entrench	-	intrench
envoy	-	envoi
flyer	-	flier
forbad	-	forbade
frenetic	-	phrenetic
fullness	-	fullness
gaol	-	jail
genuflection	-	genuflexion
gonorrhea	-	gonorrhoea
guerrila	-	guerrilla
hemophilia	-	haemophilia
indices	-	indexes
judgement	-	judgement
kerb	-	curb

lazaret	-	lazarette
lichgate	-	lychgate
likable	-	likeable
lisson	-	lissome
livable	-	liveable
loath	-	loth
lodgment	-	lodgement
lunmy	-	lunme
lychee	-	lichee-litche-licthi
marijuana	-	marihuana
mat	-	matt
machete	-	machet
medieval	-	mediaeval
milage	-	mileage
millepede	-	millipede
milometer	-	mileometer
mizzen	-	mizen
morphia	-	morphine
neglige	-	negligee
naught	-	nought
octet	-	octette
oecumenical	-	ecumenical
omelet	-	omelette
paillasse	-	pailliasse
pedlar	-	peddler
pewit	-	pewit
pouf	-	pouffe
praetor	-	pretor
premise	-	premises
primeaval	-	primeval
raccoon	-	racoon
ranee	-	rani
rase	-	raze
ratan	-	rattan

ratch	-	ratchet
ratable	-	rateable
reflection	-	reflexion
renege	-	renegue
rhomb	-	rhombus
rondeau	-	rondel
salable	-	saleable
salvage	-	salvedge
sempstress	-	seamstress
snorkel	-	schnorkel
splotch	-	splodge
stanch	-	staunch
sylvan	-	sylvan
syphon	-	siphon
teasel	-	teasel-tezzle
techy	-	tand so onhy
template	-	templet
tiro	-	tyro
tumbrel	-	tumbril
unbiasse	-	unbiased
valance	-	valence
wrick	-	rick
yogurt	-	yoghurt-yoghourt

Note that although these variant forms are archetypal parallels of the same word, caution is necessary in usage since some of the variant forms gain distinctive prominence in certain fields, locality, situation or context. For instance, although the words "indices" and "indexes" are variant plural forms of the word "index", the former is mostly applied to the field of science whereas the later is used in the field of arts.

Also, whereas the words "judgement" and "judgment" are variant forms, the former is the more commonly used while the latter is mostly used in legal proceedings and in various religious circles.

From the preceding information, it is apparent, therefore, that any attempt to the use of these variant forms without due reference to either their prominence, locality or situation of context, as the case may be, may result in unacceptable lexical item.

SPELLINGS INFLUENCED BY PARTS OF SPEECH

Many scholars are ignorant of the influence which each part of speech poses on the spelling of some English words, especially those that have to do with nouns and verbs. It is therefore, important to study the spellings below in order to avoid unnecessary spelling mistakes that border on these areas. Study the sentences, as well as in order to know how the words are used.

a) Some English words use "-c" within words to mark the noun forms while "-s" occurs in the same position to mark the verbs. Here are few examples:

DEVICE (noun)	-The computer system is a recent electronic **device**.
DEVISE (verb)	-The school authority should **devise** a means of punishing erring students.
MORTICE (noun)	-Try and produce the **mortice** to fix the planks.
MORTISE (verb)	-He has been advised to **mortise** the two beams.
ADVICE (noun)	-Mr Williams has received some pieces of **advice** from his colleagues.
ADVISE (verb)	-It is necessary to **advise** all civil servants to be law-abiding.
PRACTICE (noun)	-The **practice** of eating late in the night has become part and parcel of Bisi.

PRACTISE (verb) - The judge emphasised that lawyers should **practise** their profession freely.

b) While some words in English use "-f" in word final positions to mark their nouns, others employ "-ve" in the same position to denote the verb forms. Here are examples.

GRIEF (noun) —The incidence has caused **grief** and agony to the warring communities.

GRIEVE (verb) —The best way to **grieve** a student is to delay the release of his/her results.

BELIEF (noun) —The **belief** in traditional medicine is gradually waning away.

BELIEVE (verb) —The manager of the company will likely **believe** our story.

THIEF (noun) —You will soon be killed if you are a **thief**.

THIEVE (verb) —If you **thieve** my book, the police will catch up with you. (However, "steal" is more often used than thieve).

RELIEF (noun) —There was a great **relief** to the occupants of the house after the fire had been put out.

RELIEVE (verb) —The story was told to **relieve** the children of unnecessary tension.

DISBELIEF (noun) —His **disbelief** in the policy does not change my conviction.

DISBELIEVE (verb) —The jury had every evidence to **disbelieve** the accused person's report.

HALF (noun) —**Half** of the goods sold in the market are produced locally.

HALVE (verb) —The best way to settle the dispute is to **halve** the land in order to pacify the two brothers.

CALF (noun) —The **calf** is too tender for human consumption.

CALVE (verb) —Some cows **calve** almost yearly.

PROOF (noun) — There is no **proof** to show that the record is faulty.
PROVE (verb) — The lawyer had to **prove** the councillor's innocence in the case before he was acquitted.
DISPROOF (noun) — He presented some records as a **disproof** to his junior brother's claims.
DISPROVE (verb) — The lawyer presented genuine documents to **disprove** his claims.
REPROOF (noun) — The preacher's **reproof** for your misdeed was succinctly stated in his sermon.
REPROVE (verb) — All well-meaning citizens should **reprove** evil doers in the society.

c) Other groups of words have "-fe" for the nouns and "-ve" for the verbs at final positions. See examples below:
STRIFE (noun) — The civil **strife** to unseat the government is now over.
STRIVE (verb) — You should **strive** to obtain a good report from the company.
LIFE (noun) — Jesus came to give eternal **life.**
LIVE (verb) — Musicians normally want to **live** in the urban centres.

d) There are other sets of English words which end with "-th" to mark their noun forms but take additional "-e" to indicate verbs. Here are some examples:
BATH (noun) — The **bath** is clean enough for our guest.
You should have your **bath** now.
BATHE (verb) — It is very necessary to **bathe** before mid-day.
BREATH (noun) — The doctors have noticed that Benson's **breath** is abnormal.

BREATHE (verb)	Under normal circumstances, beings **breathe** in oxygen and send out carbondioxide.
CLOTH (noun)	Tolu's **cloth** is quite fanciful.
CLOTHE (verb)	Mrs Emem always likes to **clothe** her children soon after they had bathed.
TEETH (noun)	Clean **teeth** is a mark of good hygienic life in the family.
TEETHE (verb)	They need to **teethe** that problem before it gets out of hand.
SWATH (noun)	The **swath** in the farm can be used in feeding cows.
SWATHE (verb)	The nurse advised Thompson to **swathe** his hand in order to prevent the fracture from becoming worse.
SHEATH (noun)	It is advisable to put the machete in its **sheath** to prevent bluntness.
SHEATHE (verb)	You need to **sheathe** the knife after use.
WREATH (noun)	The **wreath** on late Adam's graveyard is quite memorable.
WREATHE (verb)	The students decided to **wreathe** the late Chief's graveyard with beautiful flowers.
SOOTH (noun)	Victor has greed in **sooth** to perform his duty.
SOOTHE (verb)	It will be decent if we can **soothe** the angry wrestler to accept defeat. (Note: This pair of words is now archaic.)

However, there is an exception to this rule as shown below:

Basic English Grammar and Usage

LOATH (adj.)	He is **loath** to work out modalities to solve problems in his family.
LOATHE (verb)	The students **loathe** going for their lessons in the afternoon.

Note: In this last case, the word "loath" is not a noun as would have been expected, but an adjective. Again, the words "blithe" and "seethe" are adjective and verb respectively. These two words have no other forms apart from these ones.

d) In other cases, some words the "-pe" at word final position to mark the nouns while they maintain only "-p" in the same position for the verb forms. See the examples below:

SLOPE (noun)	-The river behind the institution has a very steep **slope**.
SLOP (verb)	-The battery seller deliberately decided to **slop** the acid over the table into the basin.
ENVELOPE (noun)	-A well designed **envelope** helps to make a good letter.
ENVELOP (verb)	-The smoke gradually oozed out of the chimney and suddenly began to **envelop** the atmosphere, making visibility difficult.
STRIPE (noun)	-One sever **stripe** is enough to wound small child.
STRIP (verb)	-The authority of the institution may decide to **strip** him of his title if he misbehaves.

Note: There is equally an exception to this spelling form as seen in the examples given below:

SCRAP (noun)	-	Children normally litter the floor with **scraps** of paper

SCRAPE (verb) - which they use to play. The Accreditation Panel should **scrape** off any irrelevant programme from the schoolcurriculum.

Note: In the examples above, the word "scrap" is noun instead of a verb and the word "scrape" is verb instead of a noun. This indicates that there is no fixed or dogmatic rule above English spellings.

f) In final position, too, some words end with "-s" to form the noun while others with "-ze" as verbs, yet with the same root. See examples below.

EMPHASIS (noun) - The Vice Chancellor's major **emphasis** is on students passing their examination with better grades.

EMPHASIZE (verb) -The defence chief wishes to **emphasize** that "war is never won".

PARALYSIS (noun -After the diagnosis, the doctor confirmed that Janet was suffering from severe **paralysis**.

PARALYZE (verb) -It is good practice to **paralyse** evil thoughts before they have time to develop.

ANALYSIS (noun) -A synthetic **analysis** of the recent scientific theories is very essential.

ANALYZE (verb) -We will try and **analyze** the report of the panel s soon as possible.

31

g) Not that whereas the noun forms of the following words take the final "-le", the verbs take "-ll" at word final positions as shown in the following examples:

SALE (noun) - The **sale** of those stationeries has commenced some weeks ago.

SELL (verb) - Benedict wants to **sell** his new radio cassette.

TALE (noun) - The **tale** about the two legendary heroes was sane and fascinating.

TELL (verb) - I love to **tell** people what I hope to become in future.

h) Other words which exhibit similarity in terms of verb-noun relationship include the following:

PROPHECY (noun) - The recent **prophecy** about the country's future is rather bright and promising.

PROPHESY (verb) - The prophet promised to **prophesy** with sincere devotion and total loyalty.

SECRET (adj, noun) - The **secret** things belong to God. Try and keep that information secret.

SECRETE (verb) - The ductless glands **secrete** different hormones into the body system.

SIEVE (noun) - You can properly filter the tea by using a good **sieve**.

SIFT (verb) - Janet wants to **sift** the chaff

from the wheat.

i) Beside the nouns and the verbs, there are words which end with "-I" to mark adjectives but take additional "-e" to denote nouns. Here are some examples.

LOCAL (adj.) - Industries hardly thrive well in **local** areas.
LOCALE (noun) - The **locale** of the epic scene is in a very remote area.

FINAL (adj.) - Their **final** scores will determine the winner of the contest.
FINALE (noun) - The students confessed that the grand **finale** of the musical concert will remain green in their memory.

RATIONAL (adj.) - It is apparently **rational** to control prices of goods.
RATIONALE (noun) - The council wants to know the **rationale** used in selecting candidates for the election.

MORAL (adj. noun) - It is possible to maintain a high **moral** standard in a boarding school.
MORALE (noun) - The government hs decided to boost the **morale** of her army.

CHORAL (adj. - The song of the **choral** group was thrilling and memorable.
CHORALE (noun) - The **chorale** of the musician

will mark the beginning of the week-long programme.

Another unique case is with the words "proud" and "pride" as seen in the examples below:

PROUD (adj.) - The scientist likes to show off his children because he is very **proud** of them.

PRIDE (noun) - It is **pride** that robs a man of God blessings.

j) Sometimes two nouns or two adjectives so closely resemble each other that it becomes necessary to take great care to use them appropriately. Here are examples of such words:

MOOD (noun) - Mohammed was not in the **mood** to talk when I met him.
The subjunctive **mood** expresses condition and possibility.

MODE (noun) - Your **mode** of dressing is moderate and captivating.

MOTIF (noun) - One **motif** that runs through Senghor's poems is that of the "Beautiful Black Woman"

MOTIVE (noun) - His **motive** behind the action is quite unknown.

COLD (adj.) - The Northern part of the

		country experiences extreme **cold** weather during harmattan period.
COOL (adj.)	-	I prefer taking **cool** water to a chilling cold one.
HUMAN (adj.)	-	Chimpanzees sometimes exhibit **human** attributes.
HUMANE (adj.)	-	It is rare to find a **humane** military officer in the battle field.
GERMAN (adj., noun)-		The **German** language is very interesting to speakers.
GERMANE (adj.)	-	The story about Hitler is not just a fable, it provides a **germane** solution to leaders' quest for power.

Apart from the spelling areas indicated above, there are other aspects of similarity that exists between spellings of nouns and adjectives. Some nouns take on final "-nce" whereas the corresponding adjectives end with final "-nt". Here are some examples:

Adjectives	Nouns	Adjectives	Nouns
ambient	ambience	patient	patience
ambivalent	ambivalence	present	presence
brilliant	brilliance	confident	confident
radiant	radiance	dacadent	dacadence
diligent	diligence	resident	residence
distant	distance	evident	evidence
resistant	resistance	incident	incidence
indolent	indolence	reverent	reverence
lenient	lenience	silent	silence

obedient   obedience   vigilant   vigilance

However, note that "precedent" and "precedence", "correspondent" and "correspondence" are all nouns.

Equally, there are some words that resemble either possessive adjectives, pronouns or contracted forms such that it requires carefulness on the part of the user. Here are some examples of such words.

cant	-	can't
wont	-	won't
whose	-	who's
its	-	it's
your	-	you're

DIFFICULT SPELLINGS

There are many English words that pose difficulties to users partly because of the presence of letters that are not logically related to the sounds they combine to produce. At other times, the difficulties occur due to the change from one part of speech to the other.

Examine the following examples:

sustain	-	sustenance
maintain	-	maintenance
pronounce	-	pronunciation
announce	-	annunciation
denounce	-	denunciation
renounce	-	renunciation
argue	-	argument
clear	-	clarity
true	-	truly
profound	-	profundity
message	-	messenger
describe	-	description

proscribe   -   proscription
ascribe   -   ascription
generous   -   generosity
detain   -   detention
retain   -   retention

Beside the cases indicated above, there are words whose spellings are most intriguing because the initial letters are not pronounced as seen below:

mnemonic	gnome	pseudonym
gmelina	gnarled	psychology
pneumonia	gnash	psalm
pfennia	gnat	wrong
phthisis	gnau	wrangle
gnu	quay (pronounced /ki:/)	

There are other words whose spellings are very confusing. Such words include those that double their consonants and/or vowels medially or at word final positions. Here are few examples of such words:

occasion	aggressive	litter
embarrass	guarantee	boycott
catarrh	harmattan	assess
necessary	intelligent	access
diarrhoea	suppress	nobble
approach	dilemma	possess
tomorrow	occurrence	profession
scissors	haemorrhage	discreet
brassiere	gonorrhoea	proceed
resurrect	personnel	antenna
beginning	imminent	refugee
etiquette	immense	parallel
cassette	obsess	submission
settee	succeed	session

Basic English Grammar and Usage

accumulate	success	appoint
accommodate	process	arrange
unnecessary	tweeter	account
referee	twitter	profess
communiqué	tennis	mission
summary	chassis	lessen
dissent	grammar	lesson
across	interrupt	

Other examples of words with difficult spellings include those whose last letters are not pronounced. Such words include the following:

fatigue	discotheque	opaque	dialogue
cheque	critique	unique	league
rogue	physique	epilogue	plague
antique	mystique	catalogue	plaque
monologue	prologue	moustache	boutique
headache	technique	heartache	queue
brusque	colleague	clique	

It should, however, be noted that the word "communiqué" is fully pronounced and so does not follow the pattern explained above. It should be noted, too, that words with similar or almost similar medial vowels sounds cause confusion in spelling as seen below:

a) Words with "-ei" spelling:

deceive	leisure
perceive	receipt
receive	forfeit
seize	neither
conceive	either
ceiling	reign

b) Words with "-ie-" spellings:

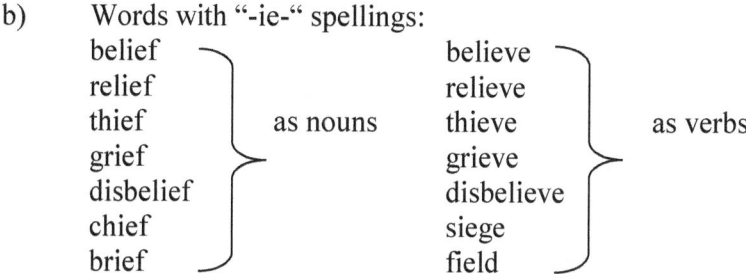

belief		believe	
relief		relieve	
thief	as nouns	thieve	as verbs
grief		grieve	
disbelief		disbelieve	
chief		siege	
brief		field	

Note that there is no verb form for the word "chief" and that the verb form for "brief" remains the same.

Beside all the aspects of spelling given above, there are various other words that pose difficulties in English spellings. Examine the words listed below:

acquaint	disciple	ledger
ascertain	disposal	bridge
acquire	distil	knowledge
obsequious	until	grudge
continuous	instil	judge
tenuous	fulfil	indulge
virtuous	hygiene	advertisement
conspicuous	trousers	thorough
incongruous	news	diphthong
exiguous	indigenous	solemn
superfluous	fundamental	column
ambiguous	fluorescent	diligent
promiscuous	forefather	interact
draught	grateful	dormitory
drought	schedule	factory
extinct	rhyme	queue
instinct	junior	cue
conjunction	lightening	rhythm
function	lightning	liaise
unction	masquerade	manoeuvre

university	measles	repertoire
varsity	plateau	etcetera (etc)
integrate	portmanteau	reprieve
entrepreneur	calender	separate
lieutenant	calendar	souvenir
soldier	weather	interact
government	whether	
environment	wether	

SPELLINGS OF IRREGULAR AND CONFUSING PLURAL FORMS

Some English spellings are influenced by plural forms of words. In pluralising the nominal class in particular, there are some nouns whose plural forms are very irregular and intriguing such that it requires tactfulness to spell such plural words correctly.

Moreover, the root of nouns either directly or indirectly affects the spellings. This is because English language, in the course of development, has borrowed words from various languages of the world and these languages predetermine the way some words are pluralised. In this section, therefore, effort has been made to group words according to their origin in order to show the similarity which they exhibit in the formation of these plural forms.

(a)   Words that are of Latin and/or Greek origin with "-sis" ending form their plurals by changing from "-sis" to "-ses" in word final position. Here are some examples.

Singular	**Plural**
apophysis	apophyses
amanuensis	amanuenses
antithesis	antitheses
basis	bases
catharsis	catharses

Singular	Plural
thesis	theses
parenthesis	parentheses
synopsis	synopses
synizesis	synizeses
syneresis	synereses
apotheosis	apotheoses
hypothesis	hypotheses
oasis	oases
stasis	stases
emphasis	emphases
psychosis	psychoses
nemesis	nemeses
neurosis	neuroses
hypnosis	hypnoses
crisis	crises
metamorphosis	metamorphoses
ellipsis	ellipses
proboscis	probosces
periphrasis	periphrases
prognosis	prognoses

It should be noted, however, that it is not every word ending with final "-sis" that must be changed to "-ses" to form its plural. For instance, words like thrombosis, chassis, exegesis re uncountable nouns and, therefore, have no other form for their plurals.

b)   Latin words ending with final "-ex" or "-ix" maintain "-xes" or change to "-ces" for their plurals forms.
The following examples are apparently true of this rule.

Singular	**Plural**
apex	apices or apexes
axis	axes
cicatrix	cicatrices

codex	codices
cortex	cortices or cortexes
index	indices or indexes
matrix	matrices
cervix	cervices or cervixes
appendix	appendices

c)   There are some set of French and Greek nouns which exhibit final "-eau" ending. Such words take additional "-x" to form their plurals. Some examples are given below:
Note, however, that sometimes only "s" is added to form the regular plural of these words, especially in American spellings.

Singular	**Plural**
Plateau	Plateaux
bureau	bureaux
beau	beaux
tableau	tableaux
trousseau	trousseaux
portmanteau	portmanteaux
gateau	gateaux
flambeau	flambeaux

Of course, it is not ever word ending with "eaux" that denotes the plural form. For instance, the word "Bordeaux" is proper noun and so does not indicate any plural form. Note also that although the French word "priendieu" ends with "-ieu", the plural form still takes final "-x" thus "priendieux".

d)   Some Latin nouns with "-us" ending only take final "-i", "a" "-ii" or "-es" for the plural while the "-us" is dropped. Here are few examples:

Singular	**Plural**
alumnus	alumni or alumna

abacus	abaci
cactus	cacti or cactuses
bronchus	bronchi
fungus	fungi
bacillus	bacilli
nucleus	nuclei
incubus	incubi
succubus	succubi
amnibus	amnibuses
focus	foci or focuses
bonus	bonuses
locus	loci
radius	radii
tarsus	tarsi
lotus	lotuses
tumulus	tumuli
stimulus	stimuli
apparatus	apparatuses
iambus	iambi
oesophagus	oesophagi
genius	genii
colossus	colossi or colossuses

However, there are few exceptions to this rule. Some Latin nouns with final "-us" have very irregular and more intriguing plural forms as seen below:

Singular	**Plural**
genus	genera
plexus	plexes
opus	opera

e) Various Latin nouns with "-um" ending take only final "-a" for their plural form while the "-um" is dropped as seen in the examples below:

SINGULAR	PLURAL
erratum	errata
agendum	agenda
interregnum	interregna
bacterium	bacteria
medium	media
corrigendum	corrigenda
minimum	minima
curriculum	curricula
dictum	dicta
quantum	quanta
millennium	millenia
auditorium	auditoria
datum	data
substratum	substrata
stadium	stadia
aquarium	aquaria
addendum	addenda
referendum	referenda
ovum	ova
ultimatum	ultimata
stratum	strata

There are equally few exceptions to this rule. Consider the following examples:

Singular	Plural
quorum	quorums
premium	premiums

f)   Some Latin and Greek nouns which end with final "-on" take only "-a" in final position while the "-on" is dropped. Here are few examples:

Singular	Plural
pleuron	pleura

Singular	Plural
phenomenon	phenomena
automaton	automata
ganglion	ganglia
criterion	criteria

g) Also, few Latin nouns ending with "-a" take additional "-e" or "-I" to form their plurals as seen below:

Singular	Plural
formula	formulae (or formuli)
antenna	antennae (antenni)
nova	novae
differentia	differentiae
novena	novenae
ulna	ulnae
tibia	tibiae
nebula	nebulae

Of course, there are exceptions to this rule, too. Some nouns with final "-a" take an additional "-s" for their plural forms as seen in the cases below:

Singular	Plural
biretta	birettas (Latin, Italian, and Spanish by origin)
arena	arenas (Latin by origin)
nova	novas or novae (Latin by origin)

h) Beside the aforementioned spelling areas, there are other complex spellings which are obviously difficult to pin down to specific spelling forms. That is, there are some words borrowed from various languages which exhibit discrete spelling patterns different from other words. There are many examples of such words as indicated below:

Singular	Plural
cicerone	ciceroni

bourgeois	the bourgeoisie
intelligentsia	the intelligentsia
monsieur	messieurs
ox	oxen
child	children
pupa	pupi
maestro	maestric
Mrs	Mmes
Mr	Messrs
Madam	Mesdames

Note that the following nouns have mutated plurals: man-men; woman-women; tooth-teeth; foot-feet; goose-geese; mouse-mice; louse-lice. These set of nouns are English by origin. The plurals in this case reflect the conventional inflection in OE.

i) Equally, compound words have diverse ways of forming plurals. Here are some specific instances.

Singular	**Plural**
autobahn	autobahnen
autodafe	autosdafe
autostrada	autostradae
billet-doux	billets-doux
man-of-war	men-of-war
passer-by	passers-by
director-general	directors-general
wagon-lit	wagons-lit
son-in-law	sons-in-law
attorney-general	attorneys-general

The rule for forming plurals in these sets of words is that the major word in the series is the one to be pluralised. Also, since these words comprise two nouns used side-by-side in each case, one usually performs a qualifying function, hence it plays the role of a modifier, particularly that of the adjective.

Note also that the following compound expressions do not take any plural forms because of the idea of collectivity and singularity which they imply:

    a six-month course
    a ten-count charge
    a four-day job
    a ten-man delegation
    an eight-member committee
    a four-year development plan
    a five-member jury
    a three-year-old politician
    a two-million-dollar project
    a twenty-kilometre journey

Observe that it is the indefinite article "a" or "an" that consolidates the idea of collectivity in the above expressions. It enhances the use of hyphen and makes the expression singular in concept and collective in meaning. Moreover, except for the head-noun, all the other expression constitute modifier elements.

However, it should be noted with utmost care that there are various words in English language which do not have the plural forms at all. For instance, the following words do not have plural forms except through the use of partitives or quantifiers:

equipment	wood	knowledge
furniture	chaos	information
staff (workers in an establishment)		grandeur
personnel	peace	tennis
aims	oil	sheep
news	rice	deer
permission	clothing	weather
sand	advice	cattle

wealth	wit	chassis
tobacco	etiquette	series
foliage	confusion	honesty
coffee	cocoa	
measles	behaviour	
conduct	character (except in a play)	
literature	evidence	

Generally, there are some basic guiding rules that can be used in classifying uncountable nouns. Here are few of such rules:

ii)   A great deal of nouns denoting compounds, substance or minerals do not have plural forms except by quantifiers, partitives or any other modifier. Study the examples below:

aluminium	enamel	silica
alum	filigree	silicate
ammonia	gold	silver
barium	graphite	sodium
basalt	grease	steel
bauxite	iron	tin ore
benzene	ivory	topaz
boron	lead	vitriol
brass	limestone	zinc
cadmium	magnesium	
caffeine	manganese	
camphor	mercury	
carbon	nicket	
catarrh	nitre	
chlorine	copper	
salt		

Most nouns indicating diseases do not take plural forms. The examples are listed below:

acne	chicken-pox	indigestion

aids	constipation	influenza
alexia	diabetes	jaundice
amnesia	diphtheria	malaria
anaemia	dysentery	myopia
asphyxia	dyslexia	paralysis
arthritis	dyspepsia	rabies
asthma	eczema	rheumatism
astigmatism	encephalitis	rinderpest
balm	epidermis	sepsis
cancer	epilepsy	

iii) Some abstract nouns with final "-nce" ending do not have plural forms except on specific cases. Here are some examples:

ambience	obedience
brilliance	prominence
confidence	providence
diligence	prudence
incidence	radiance
lenience	resistance
silence	significance
vigilance	

Note, however, that some nouns with "-nce" ending could be used both as singular and plural. Here are examples of such words
 evidence
 reference
 distance
 substance
To pluralise the nouns above, add "-s" suffix to the base

iv) Nouns ending with the suffix "-ness" rarely take the plural form. A few of such nouns are listed below:

awareness	idleness	quietness
baldness	joblessness	readiness

carelessness	kindness	selfishness
darkness	laziness	thickness
emptiness	madness	usefulness
faithfulness	neatness	vastness
goodness	yieldedness	happiness
politeness	zealousness	

The list of these set of nouns is quite a long one. Nevertheless, this rule cannot be theorised since these set of nouns do not manifest flawless perfection. For instance, there are few nouns with "-ness" suffix which can be pluralised. Here are examples of such words:
witness
sickness
illness
business
weakness

v) Nouns that suggest names of drugs do not take plural forms. Some examples are given below:

aspirin	caffeine
atabrine	Cafenol
heroin	Phensic
chloroform	grip water
chloroquin	

SPELLINGS INFLUENCED BY IRREGULAR TENSE FORMS

Some of the spellings mistakes made in written English result from the user's inability to identify the past tense and past participles of the irregular verbs. Here are few examples of such verbs:

Infinitive	**past tense**	**past participle**
arise	arose	arisen
beget	begot	begotten

do	did	done
fly	flew	flown
outride	outrode	out-ridden
partake	partook	partaken
rewrite	rewrote	rewritten
shake	shook	shaken
withdraw	withdrew	withdrawn
throw	threw	thrown

Moreso, verbs with "-ie" ending change to "-y" and then "-ing" to indicate the present participle. Examine the following examples.

vie : vying
die : dying
tie : tying
lie : lying

Note that "dye" only adds "-ing" to denote the present participle e.g. dye – dyeing

Another crucial aspect of spelling involving the change of tense form is the one that concerns consonant doubling at word final position in verbs to denote verbals or tenses. Sometimes such consonant doubling are used to indicate both the comparative and superlative degrees of adjectives or adverbs. For instance, the "lag" becomes "lagged" for its past tense or past participle and "lagging" for its present participle. The word "hot" becomes "hotter" for comparative degree and "hottest" for the superlative.

Generally, words which end in single consonant sounds preceded by a short vowel usually double the final consonant to show inflection. Relatively, in words whose final syllable is a short stressed vowel, the final consonant is repeated before a vowel suffix in order to enhance the stress of the final syllable.

The following words are cases of verbs which repeat their final consonants for the purposes enumerated above.

| annul | fit | occur | sit |
| beg | flog | overlap | skim |

begin	focus	petrol	skip
cancel	fulfil	pedal	slim
channel	grip	peg	snap
chat	gum	permit	sob
compel	gun	plan	strip
control	hop	put	stun
counsel	impel	quarrel	sum
cut	jam	quit	tag
dig	jot	quiz	tap
distill	label	recur	tar
drag	lag	refer	thud
drop	let	set	trap
drum	marvel	ship	travel
emit	model	shop	trek
enrol	nag	shun	trim
excel	nap	signal	wan
fan	net	sin	wed

The list of these set of words appears inexhaustible. Conventionally, no fixed rule is specifically attached to these spelling forms but ultimately, the following rules can be deduced from the foregoing spelling patterns.

i)   Where a single final consonant precedes a single vowel in one syllabic words, then the final consonant repeats itself to mark the present participle or other tense forms as the case may be.
See some examples below:

plan	planning	planned
sin	sinning	sinned
drop	dropped	dropped

ii)   If in a two-syllable or three-syllable word, a single final vowel is entrenched between two final consonants, then the final consonant doubles itself to indicate its participial or tense form.

Example

compel	compelling	compelled

remodel	remodelling	remodelled
signal	signalling	signalled

iii) Where a single final consonant precedes double vowel, glide or triphthong, then final consonant should not be doubled while denoting the verbal form, e.g. deem, trial, cage, and so on.

iv) Where a word ends with a vowel in word-final position, then the final vowel should not be doubled e.g. dare, fine, and so on. Generally, vowels are rarely doubled in final position to realise verbal forms. However, there could be exception e.g. skiing.

v) If a verb ends with two or more consonants, then the final consonant should not be repeated: e.g., fall, twist, prompt, and so on.

SPELLINGS OF DIMINUTIVES

Sometimes, the spellings of English words are influenced by diminutives. Diminutives refer to words which suggest smallness or a smaller size of a larger class, sense or object. It can, therefore, determine the type of spelling used for a word. Study the following examples carefully.

There are some diminutives which end with "ette," suggesting the smaller form of a bigger size. Consider the following examples:

Words	**Diminutives**
kitchen	kitchenette
statue	statuette
waggon	waggonette
case	cassette
novel	novelette
launder	launderette
cigar	cigarette
pipe	pipette
mayor	mayorette

serve   serviette
rose   rosette

There are other diminutives ending with "-ette" which do not have equivalent words for the bigger objects but still suggest "smallness" of the object or sense involved. Here are some examples:

oubliette	lazarette	burette
planchette	silhouette	courgette
roulette	vidette	corvette
moquette	mignonette	
gazette	midinette	
marionette	maisonette	
lorgnette	layette	

Note: It is not every word ending in "-ette" which serves as diminutive. The following words, for instance, are not diminutives:

etiquette	vignette
octette	brunette
sextette	briquette
palette	epaulette (epaulet)

Other words which serve as diminutives include:

leaf	– leaflet
river	– rivulet
molecule	– molecule
stream	– streamlet
lamb	– lambkin
book	– booklet
room	– roomlet

English users should, therefore, be mindful of their spellings in this area in order to use English words more meaningfully.

NOTE TO CHAPTER 2
1. Some of the spellings treated in this text are highlighted in the *Oxford Advanced Learner's Dictionary of Current English:* A.S. Hornby, Oxford University Press, 1989.

CHAPTER THREE

PUNCTUATION

Punctuation is the art of using a series of graphic, conventional marks to divide written discourses in to meaningful units. Its major purposes are:
(i) to give emphasis to expressions;
(ii) to show grammatical connection between words; and
(iii) to mark off pauses in the course of writing.

Punctuation marks vary in forms and functions, but generally, they are meant to separate one grammatical unit from the other in order to enhance clarity of meaning, orderliness of thought, and grammatical harmony within the sentence or paragraph.

The use of punctuation marks varies with individuals but all have specific purposes and distinctive principles guiding their use. These will be the major concern of this chapter. The punctuation marks that will be discussed in this unit include the following:

(i)	Full stop or period	.
(ii)	Comma	,
(iii)	Semi-colon	;
(iv)	Colon	:
(v)	Question mark	?
(vi)	Exclamation mark	!
(vii)	Dash	—
(viii)	Parenthesis or brackets	( )
(ix)	Quotation marks or inverted commas	" " ' '
(x)	Hyphen	-
(xi)	Apostrophe	'
(xii)	Ellipsis	...
(xiii)	Tilde	~
(xiv)	Braces	{ }
(xv)	Virgule	/

(xvi) Caret   ^
(xvii) Asterisk   *

The first four punctuation marks: the full-stop, the comma, the semi-colon and the colon are used to mark off varying lengths of pauses in the course of writing. The question and exclamation marks are employed to indicate inflection of voice in writing. Numbers vii, viii and ix (the dash, the parenthesis and the quotation marks) are the ones used to incorporate extra or external information into the main body of a sentence. The hyphen and the apostrophe are graphic marks used to enhance morphological processes such as formation of compound words or expressions other than the root word or word base. The braces, the ellipsis, and the tilde are used to check repetition of ideas or inclusion of unnecessary ideas, while numbers xiv, xv and xvii (the virgule, the caret and the asterisk) are variously employed to give additional information or emphasis to words, expressions or sentences. However, the last five are sparsely used in written discourses due to their scanty roles in any written work.

Of course, it should be noted that all these punctuation marks are not bound to appear in a single written discourse. The marks should, therefore, be used at appropriate instances with decency since overuse or misuse can distort meaning. Each of the punctuation marks listed above has distinctive purposes as discussed below.

THE FULL STOP OR PERIOD

The first four punctuation marks: the full-stop, the comma, the semi-colon and the colon are used to mark off varying lengths of pauses in the course of writing. The question and exclamation marks are employed to indicate inflection of voice in writing. Numbers vii, viii and ix (the dash, the parenthesis and the quotation marks) are the ones used to incorporate extra or external information into the main body of a sentence. The hyphen and the apostrophe are graphic marks used to enhance morphological processes such as formation of compound words or expressions other than the root word or word base. The braces, the ellipsis, and the tilde are used to check repetition of ideas or inclusion of unnecessary ideas, while numbers xiv, xv and xvii (the virgule, the caret and the asterisk) are variously employed to give additional information or emphasis to words, expressions or sentences. However, the last five are sparsely used in written discourses due to their scanty roles in any written work.

Of course, it should be noted that all these punctuation marks are not bound to appear in a single written discourse. The marks should, therefore, be used at appropriate instances with decency since overuse or misuse can distort meaning. Each of the punctuation marks listed above has distinctive purposes as discussed below.

THE FULL STOP OR PERIOD

The full stop or period (.) is used as an end-mark to denote the longest pause in a sentence. This is done in various ways. It is used:
    a. to mark the end of a sentence that is not a question or an exclamation, e.g. Cocks crow.
The players displayed professional skills, but no goal was scored.
    b. to indicate the end of an abbreviation, e.g. A.D., Ph.D., O.A.U., Sept.
    c. to mark a person's title and initials e.g. Rev. H.N. Beson, Rtd. Maj. Gen. A.E. Gimson.
    d. To separate units of time and money e.g. 7 a.m., 5 p.m.; ₦2.00.
    e. As decimal points to demarcate mathematical units e.g. 2.5 litres, 10.02%
    f. To mark the end of an address or date in a letter e.g.
        33 Araromi Street,

Shomolu,
Lagos.
23rd July, 1982.

g. to denote the end of a letter after the complimentary close e.g.

Yours faithfully,
Nzomo I. Nzomo.

h. to abbreviate page references in a book, e.g. p. 25; Pp. 30, 40 and 70.

Note the following are exceptions in the use of the full stop.

    a) In some abbreviations, the full stop is optional as in ie or i.e., eg or e.g., etc., viz or viz. However, current English practice is drifting towards eliminating the full stop in these set of abbreviations.

It should be noted that the full stop is optional in abbreviations such as Mr, Mrs, Dr, et al, except they occur at the end of sentence. But the user must be consistent with any of the forms s/he chooses to use.

    b) Abbreviations involving mnemonics or acronyms are not demarcated by full stops since such letter patterns are constituted into pronounceable words e.g. ASUU, ECOMOG, SOHCAHTOA, WAEC, SAN, UNESCO. However, it is not wrong if the fullstop is used.

    c) Some abbreviations involving one or two letters are not normally separated by the full stop as shown in the following examples: ₦20, ₦1m, 10k, 5kg, 20cl, 100kv, 50km.

    d) Abbreviations indicating colloquial words do not take the fullstop e.g. disco, prep, pram, dad, mum, kilo, messrs, xmas, confab.

Basic English Grammar and Usage

    e)   The full stop is unnecessary in expressions involving the abbreviation of ordinal numbers e.g. 1st, 2nd, 3rd, 4th...

    f)   Finally, symbols used to represent money do not normally take the full stop e.g. $, £, ₦, and so on.

THE COMMA

The comma (,) is the most commonly used punctuation mark in writing. It marks the shortest pause in the course of reading and writing. It is the major mark that poses great difficulties to its users. Its frugal use can give appropriate shape and meaning to a sentence. On the contrary, its misuse can cause distortion of meaning. The comma can be used in various ways to enhance clarity of expression or to give emphasis and thereby reinforce an intended meaning in a sentence. Thus, it is used at various points in a sentence in the following ways:

    a)   to mark off separate items or elements in a series e.g. Mr Okon has obtained B.Sc, M.Sc, and Ph.D in Soil Science. The milk, sugar, bread and tea are meant for your breakfast.

    b)   To set off the dependent clause from the main clause in a sentence begun by a subordinator such as if, although, since, when, while, after, unless, before, as, and so on. E.g. If I meet him today, I will speak about the issue. When we met John last Tuesday, he looked lean and sickly.

    c)   After a verbless or non-finite clause at the beginning of a sentence, e.g. Afraid and despondent, the fisherman committed suicide.
            To reap the fruit of your labour, you need to work harder.

    d)   to mark off a series of parallel clauses in a sentence, e.g. You should know that success is not easily achieved, that hardwork is the key to it, that success once achieved brings with it enduring happiness.

e) To set off the non-restrictive relative clause begun with who, whom, which, whose, and so on, e.g.
The carpenter, who repaired your furniture, has come for assistance.

f) to separate linguistic cues functioning as adverbial connectives, introductory modifiers or transitional words at the beginning or middle of sentence. Such linguistic cues include the following expressions: for instance, for example, in fact, of course, however, indeed, first of all, on the other hand, moreover, furthermore, nevertheless, accordingly, virtually, consequently, and so on. E.g.
The Federal Government has, however, decided to settle the impasse as soon as possible.
Consequently, four dialects emerged during the Old English period.

g) to mark off a series of parallel phrases in a sentence, e.g. Customs vary according to mode of dressing, form of money, manner of greeting and nature of food.

The horns blared, guns roared, and people shouted to herald the return of their famous king.
It is necessary to tell your father, your mother, your wife, and your children the whole.

h) to set off co-ordinating connectives such as but, nor, for, yet, and, or, and so on. in a compound sentence.
E.g. They looked for the girl, but she had gone home.
He should buy those items now, or it will be too late.
The weather looked stormy, yet the plane landed safely.

i) to separate modifier elements in a series, e.g.
He walked briskly, straight and decisively.
His hair was black, curly and attractive.

However, words in multiple attribution are normally arranged in the following order:

> determiner; quantifier; adjective of quality; adjective of size or shape; adjective of material or colour; noun adjunct (where applicable), and then the head-noun.

In this case, the comma should be used in the following ways:

> The two beautiful, fat, black, dancing girls are present.
> I saw a one-legged, young, mad man.

- j) to mark off elements in a direct quotation, e.g.
  After the contest, the boxer exclaimed, "We have met within the micro-ring: we will surely meet in the macro-world".
  "The case," he told the crow, "has been decided by the Panel of Enquiry".
- k) to demarcate nouns in the vocative case, e.g.
  William, you have not done your duty.
  I want to know, Mr Wahab, if you collected the tool.
  I have told them the good news, Sir.
- l) to indicate a brief stop within a sentence, e.g.
  She will like to speak to you, perhaps briefly.
  I hope to succeed in my career, God willing.
- m) to mark off contrasted elements in sentence, e.g.
  "A poet is born, an orator is made" (Cicero)
  Once bitten, twice shy!
- n) to mark off parenthetical expressions and appositive phrases in a sentence so as to give explanation or additional emphasis to an earlier expression. In this sense, the comma serves to separate interrupters in the course of a sentence, e.g.
  We saw, as it were, a horrible shadow in the moon-lit night.
  History, no doubt, evokes pathetic feelings for their plight.

o) to denote repetition of ideas which explains or reinforces an earlier word or phrase, e.g.
She advised them to be tolerant, to endure patiently.
He needed to be courageous, bold as a lion.

p) in correspondence, the comma is used:
  (i) To mark off the salutation and the complimentary close, e.g.
  Dear Uncle,
  Yours sincerely,
  (ii) The comma is also used to separate items in an address, e.g.
  33 Araromi Street,
  Shomolu,
  Lagos.
  23rd July, 1982.
  (iii) It is used to set off units of numbers in a series, e.g. 1,000; 60,000; 1,203,601
  (iv) It is also used to separate numbers in a series, e.g. 6, 12, 18, and 24 are even numbers.

THE SEMI-COLON

The Semi-Colon marks a pause that is a little longer than the comma but shorter than the full stop. In some cases, it is used instead of a comma or a full stop to achieve the desired emphasis. The semi-colon is used in the following capacities:

(a) between two or more co-ordinate clauses which are closely connected in sense but are not joined by conjunction, e.g.
He had shown remorse for his action; he should be pardoned.
He is a renowned artiste; he has the skill; he can join the troupe.

(b) to separate main clauses linked by adverbial connectives such as however, moreover, nevertheless, therefore, indeed, furthermore, on the other hand, consequently, and so on.

E.g. This kind of story is no longer fashionable; however, there are a lot to learn from it.

His attitude was repulsive and ruthless; therefore, we decided to leave immediately.

(c) to set off separate statements which contain inherent commas, e.g. When materialism, greed, hypocrisy and animosity have blinded people's eyes; when relationship is no more based on love, but on position and wealth; when politicians' utterances, attitudes, and ideas are no longer appealing to the common man; then, the best option is to pray for a change.

(d) to mark off the main clause from the subordinate clause which are related in thought but are not linked together by a conjunction, e.g.

He has advanced reasons; if his premises are considered valid, then the panel can grant his application.

(e) to denote major breaks within a sentence where the comma cannot properly be used for the same purpose, e.g.

Three reasons were advanced for his action; first, his ill-health; second, his father's death; and third, his impoverished condition.

Two prominent lawyers were involved in the case: Mr. Jim Clarence, the Lagos based lawyer; and Barrister Okoro, a renowned Senior Advocate of Nigeria (SAN).

(f) to separate statements joined by conjunctions in order to show contrast or emphasis, or to give explanation to an expression. E.g.

It is authentic to consider his plea; but by moral judgement, he is wrong.

God creates; but man procreates.

Take care of today; and tomorrow will take of itself.

(g) between a series of subordinate clauses to set up parallel structures in a sentence, e.g. If he had married before; if the wife is still alive but divorced; if he is intending to marry a new wife; then, let us know.

THE COLON

Traditionally, the colon (:) serves to denote the pause that is longer than the semi-colon but shorter than the full stop. However, there is a current trend which shows some deviation from this rule. The colon, therefore, serves the following purposes:

(a) to enumerate a long list of things introduced by such expressions as 'for instance', 'as follows', 'for example', 'such as', 'in the following', 'namely', and so on.

Lucy bought the following items: Soap, sugar, bread, cream, towel, one blouse and a pair of shoes.

We studied five subjects namely: Physics, Chemistry, Mathematics, Biology and English Language.

(b) to mark the connection between two or more co-ordinate clauses that are too closely related such that any separation will result in distortion of meaning, e.g. Mr Emerald had one daughter: she died at thirteen.

Emeka is crying: his result has been cancelled.

(c) to mark the introduction of a lengthy quotation, e.g.

Worried about the state of the society, Odili comments:

> As I stood in one corner of that vast tumult waiting for the arrival of the Minister, I felt intense bitterness welling up in my mouth. Here were silly, ignorant villagers dancing themselves lame... in honour of one of those who have started the country off down the slopes of inflation (Achebe, 1966, p.2).

It can also be used to introduce a sharp quotation. Jesus declared: "It is finished."

(d) to separate clauses that are sharply contradictory but related in sense, e.g.
God is the Creator: man is His creature.
The people upheld the decision of the council: the politicians rejected it with utmost caution.

(e) to introduce a word, a phrase or a subordinate clause preceded by a main clause in order to emphasize, explain, illustrate or affirm an earlier statement. E.g. Birth is an indispensable usher at the gate of life; it projects us to the entrance of eternity: death.
Tom has one goal, the only ambition to pursue in life becoming a doctor.

THE QUESTION MARK

The question mark (?) is other wise called the interrogation sign. It is primarily used as a terminal mark in direct speech to denote inflection of voice in writing. The major role of the question mark is to indicate the end of an interrogative statement as follows. It is:

(a) used at the end of a question requiring a reply, e.g.
Have you brought those books?

(b) used to mark the end of a rhetorical question (a rhetorical question is one asked to create an impression without necessarily requiring an answer).
E.g. Adamu, when will you become an obedient child?
Dear Lord, when will you avenge my enemies?

(c) used to denote a question that serves as a transitional statement in a discourse, e.g.
Although several premises have so far been advanced; yet, don't you think the following points will be of help to the reader?
Beside the condition outlined above, is it not necessary that we examine other conditions useful for our focus?

(d) inserted within inverted commas to mark a direct quotation. E.g. "Why did you deceive us?" Asked the Police Officer. The young man questioned: "Are you a thief?"
(e) Sometimes a question mark is optional in statements that serve either as a plea, a request or a question. E.g. Will you please inform my parents about my decision?
(f) The question mark can equally be used within parenthesis in a sentence to express doubt or uncertainty, e.g.
The renowned king ruled between A.D. 1743 (?) and 1789.
Donatello (1386? – 1466) used classical style in his work.
One of the South Eastern States (Akwa Ibom?) may soon have a refinery.

THE EXCLAMATION MARK

The exclamation mark (!) is used to express a strong emotion that is sudden or unusual such as anger, surprise, doubt or any other sudden feeling. It is used in the following instances.

(a) as an end-mark to show special emphasis at the end of an exclamatory sentence. E.g.
We had a break-through!
(b) as an end punctuation to express anger, fear, surprise or doubt. E.g.
You are mad!
In fact, it is horrible!
Oh, you mean he is dead!
He may not come today!
(c) to express words and phrases that are exclamatory, e.g. Oh! Really! Good morning! Well done!
(d) In exclamatory sentences begun with that, what and how. E.g.
That's good!
What a surprise visit!
How pretty she looks!

Note that when used with quotation marks, the exclamation mark is inserted within the inverted commas if the quoted part was shouted as in; She cried, "I am tired!"

On the other hand, if it is emphasising a strong point about the quotation, then the exclamation mark is placed outside the quotation mark. E.g.

Don't you ever say, "I am a good boy"!

THE DASH

The dash (–) is slightly longer than the hyphen. It is used:

(a) to mark an after-thought, as in:
We have decided to summon a meeting – perhaps urgently
He left the room after the sermon – a changed man.

(b) to include extra information into a sentence.
Example:
We hope to see the General Manger – he knows our plight and he will certainly help.

(c) to bring together several subjects belonging to the same verb as in:
The customs men, the police officers, the armed forces and the aviation staff – all were present at the meeting.

(d) to mark a parenthetical statement which serves as an aside or other breaks in a sentence.
Example:
Napoleon Bonaparte – so the story goes – was thrown through the window in England.

(e) to denote the climax of a situation, as in: Children screamed, men shouted, sirens blared and demons gathered – there was commotion.

(f) to give explanation to words and phrases.
Example:
The dead bodies of human beings and animals, the ramshackle of burnt houses and the deserted streets – these marked the aftermath of the violent crises.

(g) to repeat words, phrases or clauses in order to give emphasis to an expression, as in: We wanted to have a discussion – a discussion that will bring lasting solution to the problem.

PARENTHESIS OR BRACKETS

The parenthesis (otherwise called brackets) are medial punctuations inserted into a sentence, and carrying additional information which, even if removed, leaves the original sentence meaningful and complete. They are used:

(a) to introduce an explanation, an after-thought, an aside or any additional information into the main sentence.
Example:
The importance of science (whichever way one looks at it) cannot be over-emphasized.
The origin of man (of course, you cannot talk about man without referring to his history) is a very complex one.

(b) to enclose historical date within the sentence.
Example:
An important Renaissance character, Petrarch (1307 – 1374 A.D.) wrote the Italian Sonnets.

(c) to enclose page reference as in:
The whole of Unit 4 (Pp. 55-60) treats historical background.

(d) to translate into words, figure(s) of money.

Example:
He paid ₦10,000 (ten thousand Naira) for the books.

THE QUOTATION MARKS OR INVERTED COMMAS

The quotation marks can either be used singly ('...') or doubly ("..."). Traditionally, the single marks were popular with British English while the double marks were regarded as American form. But it is a current practice to use the double quotation marks for normal quotation and the single ones to denote quotation within quotation.

The quotation marks are used.

(a) to indicate direct speech.
Example
The chairman said, "I will like to inspect your unit tomorrow."
"The situation," Samson remarked, "requires immediate attention."
"How did you know that I came home?" he asked.

(b) to mark foreign words or technical terms.
Example:
"Alalok" is a popular name for cyclists.
The argument based on ignorance is technically "argumentum ad ignorantiam."

(c) to mark words or phrases that attract special attention.
Example:
There is "fire" awaiting recalcitrant workers.
You are one of the "crippling touts" in this firm.

(d) to enclose titles of books, plays, films, essays, newspapers, magazines, journals, and so on.
Example:
"Newswatch", "Daily Times", "The Blind Cyclos".

(e) to enclose quotation within quotation.
Example:
The President contended: "I view James Baldwin's statement, 'The spoils of injustice, anarchy, discontent and hatred were all around us' as our true, present condition."
Clara said: "I have come to accept that satisfaction comes through 'wringing a meaning out of meaningless life'."

It should, however, be noted that long quotations and lines of poems are normally indented and centralized in the paper used, without the quotation marks.

THE HYPHEN

The hyphen (-) is a little shorter than the dash and both are used differently. The hyphen is mainly used to enhance the morphological process involved in the formation of compound words. It is used:

(a) to form compound nouns from two separate words.
   Example:
   Director-general, key-board, eye-witness, pseudo-messiah, Court-Marshal, copy-typist, subject-matter, time-table, black-board.

(b) between a prefix and the root word ending and beginning with the same vowel or consonant respectively.
   Example:
   Pre-eminent, pre-exist, co-operate, no-one, re-echo, semi-independent, re-elect.

(c) to join fractional parts and compound numbers from 21 to 99, as in one-third, three-quarters, two-fifths; twenty-one, sixty-one, ninety-nine.

(d) with prepositions to form compound expressions.
   Example:
   son-in-law, well-to-do, wife-to-be, go-between, on-the-spot

(e) after prefixes to form group modifiers.
   Example:
   ultra-modern, post-independent, audio-visual, extra-curricular, extra-mural, post-mortem.

(f) to mark division of word at the end of the line.
   Example:
   con-sult, re-port, con-trol, repre-sent.
   (The division should, however, be done according to conventional syllable division.)

(g) before capital letters to form compound adjectives from a prefix and a proper name, as in: anti-American, post-Renaissance, all-African, Pro-June 12.

It should be noted, too, that when the hyphen is used to join a plural number with expressions involving time, money, distance, measurement, group or class, and the compound expressions formed are preceded by the article "a" or "an", then the expression produced takes singular form.

Example:
a thirty-year-old politician, an eight-year-old child, a ten-year development plan, a million-dollar project (see also spellings influenced by irregular plural nouns on page 45).

THE APOSTROPHE
The roles of the apostrophe (') are primarily two-fold:
To mark missing figures in dates or missing letters in words; and to denote the possessive or genetive case of nouns and pronouns. It is used in the following instances:

(a) to mark contracted forms of words so as to indicate omission of letters, figures or sounds.
   Example:
   doesn't (does not), can't (cannot), won't (will not), 0' clock (of the clock), '86 (1986), o'er (over), they're (they are), we're (we are), and so on.
(b) to indicate possessive forms of nouns and pronouns.

Example:
Singular nouns – wrestler's courage, Samson's letter, actor's outfit, princess' dress.
Plural nouns – Children's book, ladies' wear, among others.
Possessive pronouns – who's, one's
Indefinite pronouns – everybody's, no-one's, nobody's, somebody else's.

(c) used with "s" to form plural of letters, numbers and abbreviations, as in: stand in groups of 3's and 4's.
It happened in the 30's and 40's.
Examine the A's and B's of your letters.
You should dot your i's and cross your t's properly.

It is also used to form plural of words that do not usually have plural form. E.g.
The I's and we's have destroyed our society.

(d) to mark off proper nouns ending in "s", as in: Moses' Law, Charles' book, Jesus' ministry, among others.
Note that both forms above are mainly used in proper names.

THE ELLIPSIS (PLURAL: ELLIPSES)

The ellipsis is a grammatical device comprising three spaced periods (...) used to indicate omissions of words, phrases, clauses, a sentence or a whole paragraph needed to complete the construction or meaning of a quoted sentence, paragraph or discourse. The omitted part is usually seen as extraneous or irrelevant to the discussion or subject-matter being treated.

Example:
According to V.S. Naipaul, "The West Indian is living in a borrowed culture and ...needs writers to tell him who he is and where he stands."

However, if the ellipsis occurs at the end of the sentence, then the periods are four in number, the last denoting an end-mark to the sentence.

Example:
According to V.S. Naipaul, "The West Indian is living in a borrowed culture and as such, the West Indian, more than any other person, needs writers to tell him who he is...."

THE TILDE
The tilde (~) is merely a phonemic symbol used to mark nasalised sounds (e.g/p/). It is also a semantic symbol used by lexicographers to replace a head-word or an expression that had earlier been mentioned to avoid repetition as in: Eskimos: The ~ are very short people.

Note that this symbol cannot be really regarded as a punctuation mark because of its technical nature. It is rarely used in ordinary discourse like essays, letters, articles, and so on.

THE VIRGULE
The Virgule (/) is a diagonal mark used to separate relative or alternative expressions in a sentence.
Example:
If anybody wants to use me, he/she should pass through the necessary channels.
I will come with the file and/or the books.
The subject/verb agreement is an important aspect of study in English.

THE CARET
The caret (^) is an editorial mark used to include a piece of information that has been left out in the course of writing or printing. It is normally inserted between words to include the omitted information and is usually written just below the normal line. Sometimes it is inserted to mark correct sentence which requires more information, as in: They decided to see off the president $^{\text{and his family}}$ in a motorcade
∧

At other times, it is used to include parts of a sentence that should make it complete and meaningful.
Example:

He has spoken several ^{times to the man} about his misconduct.

THE ASTERISK

The asterisk (*) is a connotative mark used to make reference to a footnote; to call attention to something important; or to denote missing letter(s).

Examples:
The Celtic branch* of the Indo-European languages is no longer in existence.
*The languages that made up the Celtic branch include Gaulish, Cornish and Manx.
Mr J*** is coming to see you (where J*** stands for John).
Answer five* questions in all.

THE BRACES

The braces { } are marks used in printing or writing to harmonise related information sharing common syntactic units and enclosing words or figures to indicate separation from what precedes or follows it.

Example:

The $\left\{\begin{array}{l}\text{boys}\\\text{girls}\\\text{men}\end{array}\right\}$ speak good English.

CHAPTER FOUR

CAPITALISATION OF LETTERS

Capital letters play a major role in English discourse. They serve as mechanical tools with which the writer enhances concrete meaning, clarity of expression and sanity of thought. If properly used, capital letters provide rational reference points and definable link units to ideas expressed either in the sentence or in the paragraph. Their major functions are: (a) to mark the inception of sentence and direct speeches; (b) to indicate proper nouns and; (c) to denote abbreviations, among others.

Capitalisation of letters occurs in various ways. Its roles are as outlined below.

USES OF CAPITAL LETTERS

(a) Capital letters are used to begin proper nouns. Proper nouns are those nouns that mark an individual or a group off a general class of the same kind. This is done in various ways as indicated below:

    (i) Specific names of persons, titles, class or groups are normally begun with capital letters, e.g. Henry, Dr Eka, First Class (Degree), Eskimos.

    (ii) Proper names of geographical areas, towns, states, countries, continents and planets also begin with capital letters, e.g. West Indies, Lagos, Ondo State, Nigeria, Austria, Earth.

    (iii) Specific names of holidays, weekdays and months equally begin with capital letters, e.g. Easter, Friday, August.

    (iv) Also, proper names indicating religious groups, sect doctrine and personality start with capital letters, e.g. Christianity, Scripture Union, Baptism, Abraham, Adamu.

(v) Specific names of economic, political, social, traditional and educational institutions are always begun with capital letters,
e.g. Bendel Insurance Company, Social Democratic Party, Rotaract Club, Ekpe Cult, University of Ibadan.

(b) Capital letters are also used to begin the first word of a sentence, e.g. He is the president.

(c). The first letters in words indicating titles of books, newspapers, articles, poems, films, songs and movies are begun with capital letters, e.g. *Macbeth, Daily Times, The Third World Countries: Problems and Prospects, Black Woman, The Return to Mongus, Ninety Minutes in Entebe.*

In the instances shown above, the whole title may be written completely in block letters as the writer deems necessary. However, the major rule guarding capitalisation of this nature is that all major words in the title should begin with capital letters. Majors words include all nouns, adjectives, adverbs, pronouns and verbs. It also include prepositions and conjunctions with five or more letters, e.g. between, among, and so on. Note that in partially capitalised titles, articles such as "a", "an" or "the" may not be capitalised unless they occur at the beginning of the title.

(d). Capital letters are also used when writing abbreviations of proper names such as U.S.A, U.N.O., B.Sc., and so on. Initials of a person's names are normally written in capital letters: e.g. A.R. Afolabi. Acronyms, too, are usually written in capital letters, e.g. NATO, SOHCAHTOA, UNESCO.

(e). Capital letters are also used to start the first word in a direct quotation or direct speech.

Example: The boss said, "Come and see me before the close of work".

(f) Words or abbreviations denoting historical facts, historical events and specific historic documents are begun with capital letters.
Example: 450 A.D., 200 B.C., Nigerian Civil War, Warsaw Pact, Richards' Constitution, Aba Women Riot.

(g) Specific names of objects such as clothes, electronic gadgets, minerals, buildings and drugs normally start with capital letters as in Sony, Coke, Bonny Light, Manilla House, Cafenol.

(h) All proper names indicating an organisation, a company or an establishment must begin with capital letters, e.g. West African Examination Council, Coca Cola Bottling Company, Federal Radio Corporation of Nigeria, and so on.

(i) The pronoun 'I' is normally written in capital letter regardless of the position which it occurs in the sentence. E.g. I will come tomorrow. You and I will be needed there.

(j) Adjectives derived from proper nouns should begin with capital letters, e.g. Mosaic law, African culture, Darwinian theory.

(k) Proper names in the genetive case used as modifiers should begin with capital letters as in, Thompson's book, Sophocles' *King Oedipus,* Ibsen's *Wild Duck.*

(l) Names of languages spoken in any part of the world should begin with capital letters as in: Hausa, Swahili, English, Ibibio, Anaang, Igbo, Urhobo, Yoruba, and so on.

(m) Words denoting interjection or exclamation should begin with capital letters. E.g. Ah, I am very surprised! Help me, Oh God!

(n) Biblical names and pronouns referring to God, Jesus Christ or the Holy Spirit should begin with capital letters, e.g. Let God avenge His enemies.
Jesus told His disciples that He is coming again.

Also, names of sacred figures or places should begin with capital letters. E.g.
>Arabian Knight, Diana of the Ephesians, Mount Olive.

(o) All names of subjects or titles of courses studied in schools as well as certificates issued in institutions of learning normally begin with capital letters. The examples are as follows: Physics, Electrical Engineering, First School Leaving Certificate, Doctorate Degree (Ph.D).

(p) Names denoting specific classes in school are begun with capital letters e.g. Form IV, JSS III, SS II, Part IV.
Designated classes are written in capital letters, too.

(q) Proper names denoting addresses – names of roads and streets usually start with capital letters as in Azikiwe Avenue, 25 Omoniyi Street, Lagos Lane.

(r) Capital letters are also used to begin the first words in salutation and the complimentary close in letter writing as in Dear Sir, Yours faithfully.

(s) Specific names of animals and birds equally start with capital letters e.g. Blackie (a dog), Tom Tom (a bird).

CAPITALIZATION OF HOMONYMS

All proper nouns should begin with capital letters. However, there are some words that are the same in form and sound to another but have different meanings. Such words are called homonyms. Some homonyms occur as proper nouns while their counterparts either function as common nouns or another part of speech.

In this case, it is the capital letter that makes the difference. Scholars are, therefore, cautioned to use the right letter to begin such homonyms. Homonyms functioning as proper noun should thus begin with capital letters. Examine the following words and how they are used in sentences:

Basic English Grammar and Usage

August (noun)	-**August** is the eighth month of the year.
august (adj.)	-The president was once our **august** visitor.
Eve (noun)	-**Eve** was the first woman to live on earth.
eve (noun)	- If the ANC gave up the struggle at the **eve** of independence in South Africa, then the entire Black race would have been disappointed by her action.
Frank (noun)	-The **Frank** was a very formidable tribe that existed in about the 6th century A.D.
frank (adj.)	-Clement is always very **frank** to tell his friend the truth.
God (noun)	-**God** is the creator of the universe.
god (noun)	-The **god** of money has plunged the world into inexplicable corruption.
Japan (noun)	-**Japan** is likely to be the world's largest producer of electronic gadgets.
japan (verb)	-If you **japan** that equipment, it will appear more attractive.
Job (noun)	-Job is a biblical character who is well known for his patience
job (verb)	-I would like to start **job** immediately after my education
May (noun)	-The month of **May** usually marks the beginning of winter in some parts of the country.
may (verb)	-You **may** not bother to go to school today because of your ill-health.

Mercury (noun)	-The students contended that **Mercury** will ever remain the closest planet to the sun.
mercury (noun)	-Inside the thermometer, there is a little quantity of **mercury** to aid the measurement of temperature.
Mosaic (adj.)	-The **Mosaic** law was the best at its time.
mosaic (noun)	-Generally, **mosaic** arts seem to be more durable and attractive.
Peter (noun)	-At the conference hall, **Peter** sat close to the president.
peter (verb)	-The election materials may likely **peter** out if no new supplies are made soon.

However, note that if the second words beginning with small letters occur at the beginning of a sentence, then they are begun with capital letters. To capitalise letters appropriately, one needs to have a concrete knowledge of the letters of alphabet. This may appear demeaning, but it is very essential. Study the letters below and note the differences between the small letters and the capital letters respectively:

Aa Bb Cc Dd Ee Ff Gg Hh Ii Jj Kk Ll Mm Nn Oo Pp Qq Rr Ss Tt Uu Vv Ww Xx Yy Zz

It should be noted, however, that except six alphabets (j,k,v,w,y and z), all the other twenty English alphabets were originally Latin alphabets.

CHAPTER FIVE

THE PARAGRPH

Meaning and Function

In a normal rank-scale (i.e. the hierarchy of the units of linguistic description), the morphemes function as the constituent of words; words function as the constituent of phrases while clauses are direct constituents of the sentence. Closely following the sentence in the rank-scale is the paragraph. According to Oluikpe (1981, p.209), the paragraph is the largest single unit of an essay. The paragraph, therefore, is the largest single division of a piece of writing containing one or more sentences which deal with one central idea. Each new paragraph usually begins on a separate line.

The major role of the paragraph is to develop a single unit of thought at a time. Thus, the paragraph picks up a single theme and discusses it separately and exhaustively. This serves to enhance transition of thought, disparate unit of idea and step-by-step development of the discussion. The terminal mark of the paragraph is the full stop while its inception is marked by the sign of indentation.

Indentation is the practice of starting the first word in a line of print or writing farther from the margin than the others. It is the commonest mark of the paragraph (although there are other indexes of the paragraph as will be discussed under types of paragraph). All the discussions within the paragraph are hinged on a single sentence - the topic sentence.

The Topic Sentence

The topic sentence is a **sentence** (not a topic per se) that expresses the central point or the dominant idea in the paragraph. If properly employed, a topic sentence registers the purpose and meaning of any single paragraph. It thus serves as a spring-board upon which the whole paragraph rests for its meaning. Virtually, the topic sentence expresses a central thought which binds up a group of related sentences. All the other sentences in the paragraph merely depend on the topic sentence for their meaning.

The position of the topic sentence is usually a conspicuous one. Its presence is normally marked by a concrete, precise and clearly stated sentence usually placed at the beginning, the middle or the end of a paragraph. The remaining sentences merely serve to expand or elaborate on the point raised in the topic sentence.

The basic purpose of the topic sentence is to epitomise the main point raised in the paragraph. This gives the reader a sense of direction on the trend of the discussion in each paragraph. The entire effect of the topic sentence is to enhance clarity of expression, unity of meaning, coherence of thought and effectiveness of the paragraph. Following the topic sentence are usually series of accompanying, supporting sentences that further explain or complement the idea emphasised in the topic sentence. However, these cannot be accomplished without certain definable qualities as discussed below.

THE QUALITIES OF A GOOD PARAGRAPH

There are certain distinctive qualities that contribute to the uniqueness of any particular paragraph. These include unity, coherence, clarity, simplicity, precision, completeness and legibility. Each of these qualities has an unparalleled part to play in the development of each paragraph in particular, and the essay, letter or discourse in general. A detailed treatment of these qualities is, therefore, indispensable to our discussion in this unit. Let us now examine each of the qualities in turn.

Unity: This implies that a single paragraph should deal with one main point or topic at a time. Nothing should be introduced to a paragraph unless it is relevant to the discussion in the paragraph. A single idea should be given a paragraph and the point in that paragraph developed to form a complete unit of thought. All sentences within the same paragraph should harmoniously lead to a central idea. This eases comprehension and summary.

Coherence: This deals with the co-ordination of sentences and paragraphs in any discourse. The sentences in the paragraph should form a series of interrelated units of information leading naturally to a central idea. In others words, a coherent paragraph should be homogeneous in subject-matter and orderly in content. Thus, coherence evolves a technique that can give a sense of direction to the reader to follow the writer's trend of thought from the beginning to the end of the discussion. Lack of co-ordination of this nature makes comprehension difficult and leaves the sentence or paragraph in "distorted overcoat".

Coherence could be enhanced through the use of some linking devices such as linguistic cues and transitional expressions. Such devices act as linguistic sign-posts or directional signals to the reader. Here are some useful **examples:**

(a) to indicate purpose in a discourse, the following expressions are appropriate: for the purpose, with this end in view, to this end.

(b). to mark contrast, use the following expressions: but, yet, however, nevertheless, on the contrary, on the other hand, not withstanding.

(c). to enhace a logical conclusion, use expressions such as consequently, as a result, therefore, thus, accordingly, hence, so, and so on.

(d). to show comparison, the following expressions are suitable: similarly, likewise, in similar fashion, in like manner.

(e). to denote time, use soon, after, meanwhile, immediately, at this point, at first, then, now, soon, in the mean time, gradually, later.

(f). to make an illustration, the following are appropriate: for instance, for example, to illustrate.

(g). to mark continuity of thought, use furthermore, moreover, in fact, indeed, of course, again, also, in addition, likewise, next, besides, then, in other words.
(h). to summarise a point, use the following expressions: in short, all in all, to sum up, to conclude, finally, in sum, laconically, succinctly, in conclusion.
(i) to make an enumeration of facts, the following are possible expressions: first, second, third, ..., to begin with, in the first place, finally, also, moreover, furthermore.

Any of these expressions should be used to mark specific instances as the case may be for the purpose of developing the paragraph or a whole discourse.

Clarity: This implies the use of vivid expressions to say exactly what the writer has in mind. Here, one should be careful to avoid the use of confusing words and words that suggest exaggeration. The paragraph requires the use of plain, fresh language to enhance clear and meaningful expressions.

Simplicity: The use of simple, straight-forward but logically constructed sentences to express ideas helps to enhance the reader's understanding of a discourse without "an interpreter". It is more helpful to employ simple, correct words and sentences alongside with familiar illustrations to give vivid description or explanation to the points raised in a discussion than to use pointless elaboration alongside with high-sounding, or verbose expressions.

Precision: Precision implies that the sentences in the paragraph should be brief and straight to the point. The writer should avoid the use of verbose or abstract expressions as well as long, winding sentences. Unsuitable idioms should be kept at bay. In other words, the paragraph should contain as few words as are necessary to express ideas. In fact, Gowers (1948,p.80) cautions: "use no more words than are necessary to express your meaning". Unnecessary repetition of words, expressions or ideas should be avoided as much as possible. It should be noted that too many-worded paragraph with series of repeated ideas irritates even a patient reader. Ideas should, therefore, be tersely expressed and clearly stated.

Completeness: Meaningful and wholesome ideas should be developed both in the sentences that make up the paragraph and the paragraphs that form a single discourse. The idea expressed in each sentence should be complete in sense and the sentences in each paragraph of the discourse should develop one complete unit of thought. Of course, it should be noted as well that an incomplete paragraph ultimately gives a disunited picture of what should have naturally been constituted into a lofty discourse.

Legibility: This is another important but negligible quality of a good paragraph in particular and an essay, a letter or a discourse in general. If it is handwritten discourse, the handwriting should be easily readable. Even in printed materials, the printing should be legible too. A legibly handwritten or printed material makes comprehension easier, faster and more interesting. A well-formed handwriting or printed characters lures the reader to go through the material with mounting interest.

However, these qualities may not count much if the writer does not acquire adequate knowledge of the various methods that can be employed in developing any particular paragraph according to its content and scope. This, therefore, necessitates the discussion on the methods of developing the paragraph.

Methods of Paragraph Development

A writer of an essay, letter or any other formal discourse may use one or more of the following techniques to develop each paragraph of the write-up at a time.

Comparison: The writer may employ the techniques of comparing opinions or facts while at the same time dividing the theme(s) of the discussion into meaningful and wholesome units. This helps to widen the scope of the discussion in the paragraph.

Use of question: The paragraph may also be developed through giving an answer to a thought-provoking question posed at the beginning of the paragraph. Such questions may be regarded as the topic sentence in that paragraph.

Cause and effect approach: Through the technique of cause and effect, a writer can expand ideas by presenting logically certain instances or situations that have engendered the emergence of others. This technique demands orderly presentation of premises and logical advancement of valid conclusion.

Definition: A writer may, in descriptive, expository or explanatory discourse, use the technique of defining the terms used in the discussion. This makes room for clarity and by so doing, eliminates undue ambiguity and prevents misinterpretation.

Illustration: Illustrations comprise accompanying information meant to serve as supporting facts to an assertion, opinion or an earlier stated information. Sometimes, illustrations are used to establish the ideas raised in the topic sentence. Through this technique, a writer can develop many paragraph s on a single subject of discussion.

Description of details: In expository or descriptive discussions, details are required in the information given. The technique is, therefore, used to expand ides through giving of minute, but essentially distinctive information to aid the reader.

Classification of ideas: This method is not an uncommon one. The essence is to build up ideas into harmonious units of thought so as to show major sub-divisions, and thereby, help the reader to receive already classified information. This technique helps the writer to develop each paragraph with near perfection. This is because each classified information is fully developed in a paragraph before another point is considered for discussion.

Of course, the discussion on any particular paragraph partly depends on the type of paragraph developed. This is why it is necessary to examine types of paragraphs as a separate unit.

Types of Paragraph
Paragraphs vary according to the pattern they occur. Some paragraphs occur in indented form as mentioned earlier. This is the major form used in many Nigerian textbooks presently. It is used in essay writing, letters, seminars papers, thesis, project – to mention just a few. There are other kinds of paragraph, namely:
1. blocked paragraph;
2. hanging paragraph; and
3. headed paragraph

Blocked paragraph
In blocked paragraph, writing begins at the same vertical point in the printed or writing material. The only remarkable feature of this form is that a line is normally skipped before starting the next paragraph.

Example:
This is to inform all staff of this Association that the screening exercise will take place between Monday, 25th September, 1992 and Tuesday, 3rd October, 1992. The venue is the Banquet Hall of the Association.

On the basis of the above information, therefore, all staff are expected to come to the venue for the screening exercise with all valid documents and credentials. The physical presence of each staff is of paramount importance, and late-coming will not be tolerated.

Hanging Paragraph
In hanging paragraph, the first word of the paragraph begins on the left hand margin of the line while the subsequent lines leave uniformed space behind the starting point of the first line.

Example:
This is to inform all staff of this Association that the screening
    exercise will take place between Monday, 25th September,

1992 and Tuesday, 3rd October, 1992. The venue is the Banquet Hall of the Association.

On the basis of the above information, therefore, all staff are expected to come to the venue for the screening exercise with all valid documents and credentials. The physical presence of each staff is of paramount importance, and late-coming will not be tolerated.

Headed Paragraph

The headed paragraph s are mostly used in correspondence such as enquiry letters, orders, request letters and reports. When there are series of divergent information put together in a particular discourse, decency demands that separate pieces of information be itemized for easy identification under separate sub-headings.

Example:

Purchase of Office Equipment

Our organisation has decided to purchase heavy equipment during the month of July, 1992 at the cost of N20m. The Bursar had equally been directed to release money for the purchase accordingly.

Sales of Office Furniture

The officials of the organisation have agreed to sell some of the less useful office furniture on 20th August, 1992. The proceeds from such sales will be used to purchase new ones.

It should be noted strictly, that, of all these kinds of paragraphs, the most commonly used in the Nigerian context is the indented paragraph. An example of the indented paragraph could be seen below:

This is to inform all staff of this Association that the screening exercises will take place between Monday, 25th September, 2014 and Tuesday, 3rd October, 2014. The venue is the Banquet Hall of the Association.

Caution: Students who are taking the SSCE and NECO examinations are advised to use this last type for all kinds of essays, letters and other formal discourse. Students in higher schools, except otherwise instructed should also use the indented style of paragraphing.

Length of the Paragraph

Generally, there is lack of uniformity in the length of paragraph s in any write-up. While some paragraph s may be long others may be relatively short. In fact, some paragraph s may contain just a single sentence which only takes between one and three lines. The length of the paragraph, thus, depends on how much information is needed to develop a full-fledged idea within the paragraph. It also depends on the dexterity, style or convention adopted by the writer, or sometimes, on the subject-matter and expressive ability of the essayist.

In essence, each point or idea raised in each paragraph should be adequately treated or fully developed so as to enhance the intended meaning. The length of each paragraph depends on whether the point had been exhaustively discussed. Too long paragraphs should, however, be avoided since it may contain so many facts than necessary. Relatively, too short paragraph s present scanty facts such that the meaning of the entire paragraph may be distorted as a result of this. A paragraph should then be moderate – not too long and not too short. If a single paragraph has too many facts in it, the paragraph can be authentically split into two for the sake of convenience. But, there are also some peculiar paragraph s that require unique treatement as discussed below.

Special Purpose Paragraphs

There are some specific paragraph s in any write-up that require special treatment. They are meant to give special information about the discourse or to indicate the direction under which pieces of information are to be relayed.

The special purpose paragraph s include the following:
1. introductory paragraph;
2. transitional paragraph;
3. narrative paragraph;
4. developmental paragraph; and
5. concluding paragraph.

The Introductory Paragraph

The introductory paragraph has a distinctive role in any discourse. Its functions are:
(i) to arouse the interest of the reader;
(ii) to show the direction or line of reasoning under which the discussion will be considered; and
(iii) to introduce the subject matter of the discussion.

It should be noted, however, that the introduction does not show the main facts of the discourse. Rather, it provides a skeletal picture which serves as a guide to the reader on the author's trend of thought in the course of the discussion.

A discourse could be introduced in one of the following ways:

(a) by giving the definition of unfamiliar or less familiar terms as applied to the subject of discussion.

Example:

On "Shakespearean Tragedy", the introductory paragraph could begin as follows:

The word "tragedy" is very often used loosely to describe any disaster or misfortune. It can be used to refer to a work of art, usually a play or novel, in which disaster overtakes the hero. Precisely, Shakespearean tragedy probes with high seriousness questions concerning man's existence and his experience in the universe. Its roles are numerous.

(b) by projecting a brief adage, allusion or anecdote related to the subject matter.

Example:

On the topic, "History of the Nigerian Nation", the following adage may apply

"The history of today started somewhere yesterday, and the events of today constitute tomorrow's history". The historical setting of the Nigerian nation is a long and winding one. It started with the coming of the colonial masters in the 19th century. The entire episode has divergent versions and each is important for consideration.

(c). by advancing a thought-provoking question on the subject of discussion.

Example:

On the subject, "Violence in the Third Republic", the following introduction could be suitable.

Who would have thought that some unscrupulous politicians will re-introduce violence into the politics of the Third Republic? The recent clashes between factions of the two main political parties constitute an indecent development in our national politics. It is high time we looked closely into the causes of this unwholesome situation with a view to correcting it.

(d). by using an apt quotation on the subject-matter.

Example:

On the topic, "Political Crises in the Third World Countries", the following introduction is appropriate:

"Power corrupts and absolute power corrupts absolutely". The political practice in many third world countries – African and Asian countries alike – allows little or no room for sharing of power. This trend of development has eventually engendered the various crises that have rocked the Third World countries for more than four decades now. It is, therefore, necessary to examine the causes, effects and possible remedial measures to curb this inordinate development.

(e). by making a direct statement on the subject.

Example:
On the subject, "The Merit of Scientific Inventions", the following introduction is suitable:
Comfort is the aim of science. There have been several scientific inventions over the past few decades. More sophisticated medical equipment have been developed and many delicate surgical operations have been carried out more effectively. The space-crafts, scud and patriot missiles as well as the recent invention of the computer system are the major landmarks in the history of scientific development. In fact, the various merits of scientific inventions are more pronounced in recent years and it is necessary to look at these merits in turn.

(f). by raising contrasting views on the subject-matter.
Example:
In "Nigeria Should Depend More on Agriculture Than on Oil", the following introduction may apply:
The bane of the nation's economy depends more on internally generated revenue than on external resources. Various quarters of the Nigerian society have offered rational suggestions on what the nation should depend upon for a viable national economy. While some have based their premises on effective agricultural systems, others have harped on total dependence on oil revenue. My view, however, is close to midway except for some few constraints that seem to pull more weight on agriculture which I wish to support unequivocally. There are several determiners of this choice.

(g) by making a general statement on the subject-matter.
Example:
On the topic, "The Roles of AU in African Development", the following introduction can apply:
The strongest continental organisation in Africa today, the African Union (AU), initially known as

Organisation of African Unity (OAU), was founded at inception by thirty African Heads of State and governments in Addis Ababa, Ethiopia, on May 23, 1963. Its major goal was to serve as an inter-African organisation aimed at serving the interest of independent African countries and working for progress. Initially, efforts were thwarted by political, linguistic and economic differences among member nations. But recently, these barriers have given way to more progressive roles which the organisation plays in the continent. These roles are numerous.

Note: Although the introductions set out in these cases seem to be moderate enough, there could be other introductions which may require between three and five lines of the writing material to make it complete and meaningful. Moreover, others may be more lengthy than the ones illustrated above.

The Concluding Paragraph:

The concluding paragraph is another unique unit of any discourse. It emphasises, and thereby, affirms the main points raised during the discussion. This, it does in summary form. It is the paragraph that establishes tersely and more vividly the principal points treated during the discussion.

The concluding paragraph may begin with a periodic sentence. A periodic sentence is one that keeps the reader in suspense until the end of the sentence. "It normally builds up, often through two or more parallel constructions, to a climatic statement in the final main clause" (Macrimmon, 1972,p.134).

Example:

The conclusion on "Political Crises in the Third World Countries" may take the following form.

That Third World politics is still a baby of circumstance is an impeccable truth; that a change of the situation in the nearest future seems impossible is pitiful; and that the leaders of these nations can avert total collapse in Third World politics is an inevitable logic; therefore, the door of innovation is still open for a change, and without delay.

Another viable conclusion with a loose sentence on the same topic can take this form:

It is clear from the aforementioned instances that the crises in Third World politics is heading for a crash. The leaders of Non-Aligned Nations should act without delay to avoid a very obscene situation in Third World politics.

The Transitional Paragraph

The transitional paragraph is normally a short one. In most cases, it does not necessarily have an outstanding topic sentence. It is basically used to effect a change from one section of a discussion to another in order to introduce a new idea to be treated in the subsequent paragraphs.

Example:
The following may function as the transitional paragraph on the topic: "The Importance of Cereals in the Nigerian Economy."

Having discussed several varieties of cereal available in Nigeria, let us now examine the roles played by these set of crops in our national economy.

The Narrative Paragraph

The narrative paragraph is particularly used when telling a story or narrating an incident. Most of the times, this type of paragraph is interwoven with other type of paragraph presented in a story-telling mood. Generally, it is usually longer than the normal paragraphs because each narrative paragraph contains specific details of the incidence relayed or described.

Example:
As he passed by the box, the walker put his hand on his right trouser pocket and pulled out the debris of used tickets and threw everything on the heap. At the curve on the road, he stopped a while, his gaze directed downward

as if he was trying to make up his mind about something. When he began to cross over to the other side of the road, his eyes were still fixed on the tar in front of him, and he walked quite slowly (Armah, 1968, p.9).

The Developmental Paragraph
This type of paragraph usually derives from other paragraphs, particularly, the introductory paragraph. It is normally the paragraph that takes on from where the writer left off in his last statement or remark in the preceding paragraph. Its goal is to give explanation or develop the point which a writer has just provided clues to in the paragraph just before the new one begins.

Pitfalls to Avoid in the Development of Paragraph
There are may loophole that should be avoided when developing the paragraph of essays, letters or any other write-up. Here are some of them;
1. Use of informal, archaic or confusing expressions.
    These occur in various ways as outlined below:
    (i) Use of slang e.g. chop, biz, gonna, wanna, crazy.
    (ii) Use of archaisms i.e obsolete words that are old and out of use e.g. beseech, tiding, unto, forward, beget, damsel.
    (iii) Use of colloquial expressions, i.e. informal expressions and short forms of words, e.g. specs, disco, exam, matric, cos, tho, confab, prefab, maths, dad, mum, and so on.
    (iv) Use of jargons i.e., "big" or technical discourse.
    (v) Use of foreign and uncommon expressions e.g. ipso facto, sine qua non, and so on. in an ordinary discourse.
    (vi) Use of clichés or hackneyed expressions i.e stereo-type phrases, ideas or expression that had been over-used until its meaning becomes obsolete.

- (vii) Use of padding, i.e. too many words without creating impact in hope of filling an empty space.
- (viii) Use of malapropisms i.e. misuse of words e.g. cannon for canon, discreet for discrete, desperate for disparate, discuss for discus, and so on.
- (ix) Use of redundant expressions or tautology i.e. needless repetition or duplication of words or phrases without making additional meaning, e.g. basic essentials, consequent results, collapse and fall, absolutely complete, priceless and invaluable, so therefore, still or yet still.
- (x) Use of vogue words i.e. expressions that are quite new and have not yet been recorded in the dictionary, legebenz, bookamania, frenemy, and so on.

2. Tact should be applied in making generalisations, particularly in relation to absolute terms or indefinite pronouns such as everybody, all, nobody, everyone, no-one, never, always, everything. If not properly used, these expressions can result in confusion and misinterpretation of the message relayed.
Example: All Nigerians know the truth.
(Does this include infants, mad men, and so on. in Nigerian?)

3. Candidates should avoid the use of high-sounding words except when they are typically important. For instance, use 'fire out-break' instead of 'conflagration', 'big' instead of 'gigantic', and so on., except where the alternative expressions provide the more desired meaning or effect.

4. Idiomatic expressions should be used sparsely in a single discourse. Too many idiomatic expressions used in a single paragraph cripples the ideas expressed in that paragraph or discourse.

5. Except on letters (where applicable), candidates should avoid too many use of personal pronouns such as I, we, us and even 2nd and 3rd person pronouns, such as you and they.

Also, unnecessary use of gender and number or shifts from one person, or tense to another should be guarded against.

Example:
   (a) One hopes that an effective speaker is a good person but you cannot prevent a bad person from performing evil deeds and speaking corrupt words.
   (b) The School Board meeting was duly held but no agreement was reached.

   In sentence (a) above, either 'you' or 'one' may go with an appropriate concordial element provided there is consistency with the pronoun chosen by the writer.

6. Avoid incomplete construction such as: The players displayed remarkable skill but no goal. They abandoned the scene which they decided to look.

7. Ambiguous expressions should be avoided as much as possible.

Example:
"*I saw the thief run through the key-hole.*"

There are two interpretations to this statement: it is either the person saw the thief mysteriously running through the key-hole or that he looked through the key-hole and then saw the thief running away. This latter meaning (which is supposed to be the intended meaning) is rather implied than stated, and so nebulous.

Relatively, the statement: "*Flying planes are dangerous,*" could be misleading. It either means that the act of flying planes is dangerous or the planes that are flying could be dangerous. Therefore, candidates should be very careful to say exactly what they mean.

8. Also, scholars should avoid the error of comma splice. This means the use of comma instead of period or semi-colon between main clause not linked by a co-ordinating conjunction.
   Example:
   *We have spoken to him, he will likely come tomorrow.
   *She is pretty, the mother talks about her always, she is aware of this.
   In these sentences, the commas are wrongly used to punctuate where the full-stop or conjunction could have been more appropriate. Here are the correct versions of these expressions:
   We have spoken to him and he will likely come tomorrow.
   She is pretty and she is aware of this because the mother talks about her always.

9. The use of run-on sentences should be avoided in the paragraphs, too. Run-on sentences are very long sentences strung together or packed with so many ideas embodied in a single sentence.
   Example:
   There have been so many organisations registering for the competition and they are prepared to win prizes even though there is little or no suspicion on who will finally win the three gold medals available and take the glory home without any hitch from the sponsoring bodies.

10. Candidates should also avoid the use of dangling modifiers in sentences. Dangling modifiers are those modifiers that do not clearly relate to some word in the sentence. Usually, in a dangling modifier, when a referent is omitted, the performer is often left out, making the sentence almost meaningless.

Example:
- (a) Discouraged by their performance, the cassette began to sing melodiously.
- (b) Expecting the strangers, the food was ready by 6 p.m.

The sentences above can be corrected thus:
- (a) Discouraged by their performance, the coach began to play the melodious music in his radio cassette.
- (b) Expecting the strangers, the host made sure that the food was ready by 6 p.m.

CHAPTER SIX

HOMOPHONES AND OTHER CONFUSING WORDS

Homophones are words with similar or almost similar pronunciation, but which are different in meaning, spelling or origin. Homophones and other confusing words constitute one of the major problems which students encounter in the study of English Language. Many homophones are common ones, which could be easily detected by English learners. Others are almost very difficult to notice. The difficult ones are, therefore, the major concern of this chapter. There is an attempt to transcribe, phonemically, each of the words used to illustrate homophones. In doing this, the authors have adopted Gimpson (1994), Trask (1996) and Hornby (2010) as models for optimal results.

WORDS	TV	POS	MEANING(S) OF THE WORDS
altar	/ˈɔːltə/	N	Raised platform in the church; a secluded place of worship.
alter	/ˈɔːltə/	V	To change, modify or adjust.
utter	/ˈʌtə/	adj. V	Complete, total, absolute, or entire. Say, speak, pronounce.
accent	/ˈæksənt/	N; V	Prominence, stress; to pronounce with accent
ascent	/əˈsent/	N	The act of climbing up or ascending.
assent	/əˈsent/	N; V	Acceptance or approval; to approve
access	/ˈækses/	N	Right to something; way to a place
assess	/əˈses/	V	Examine, evaluate; to appraise or examine.
artist	/ˈɑːtɪst/	N	One skillful in Fine or Literary Arts; a professional in Fine Arts.
artiste	/ɑːˈtɪst/	N	A professional singer, dancer, actor/actress

attach	/əˈtætʃ/	V	To fasten or join two or more things or persons together.
attaché	/əˈtætʃeɪ/	N	A personnel attached to an ambassador.
behalf	/bɪˈhaːf/	N	For or in the interest of (usually on behalf of or on his/her/my behalf).
behave	/bɪˈheɪf/	V	To act or conduct oneself; function or work.
boarder	/ˈbɔːdə/	N	A lodger or one who squats with another; a student at a boarding school.
border	/ˈbɔːdə/	N, V	Line of demarcation between two state or countries, edge; to resemble or be close
bother	/ˈbɒðə/	V	To trouble, worry or cause to be nervous.
breadth	/ˈbretθ/	N	Width; distance between two different sides.
breath	/breθ/	N	The act of inhaling and exhaling air; air breathed in.
breathe	/briːð/	V	Verb form of the noun "breath".
cannon	/ˈkænən/	N	A heavy stationary gun usually fixed to the ground.
canon	/ˈkænən/	N	Church or ecclesiastical law or decree particularly designed for the Christian priests.
canvas	/ˈkænvəs/	N	A kind of tough material or rough cloth used for shoes, bags, sails, tents, and so on.
canvass	/ˈkænvəs/	V	To campaign for votes or ask for political or social support.
calvary	/ˈkælvərɪ/	N	The place where Jesus was crucified on the cross.
cavalry	/ˈkəvlrɪ/	N	Military personnel or soldiers who fight on horse back
cession	/ˈseʃn/	N	The legal act of agreeing to give up one's

section	/ˈsekʃn/	N	property, rights or claims. A small group of a larger class, an apartment, a small portion of a whole
session	/ˈseʃn/	N	Part of a school year or term; time occupied by a meeting; a meeting period in an organization
charlady	/tʃɑːˈleɪdɪ/	N	A female cleaner in an office or a public building.
chairperson	/tʃeˈpɜːsn/	N	A woman who presides over a meeting or an occasion.
chapter	/ˈtʃæptə/	N	One of the major divisions or sub-divisions of a book, magazine or thesis; a major part of something.
charter	/ˈtʃɑːtə/	N, V	Right or permission to use something; to give right or privilege to do or use something.
chatter	/ˈtʃætə/	N, V	Quick unimportant conversation; quick rapid sounds made by animals; to chatter.
circular	/ˈsɜːkjʊlə/	Adj.	A notice passed round to give information; of a circle, round.
secular	/ˈsekjʊlə/	Adj	Corporeal, mundane, of the world, not spiritual
cite	/saɪt/	V	To mention or quote something or somebody as a point of reference, an example or an instance of support.
site	/saɪt/	N	Place or location where something takes place or location where building is set up.
sight	/saɪt/	N, V	The act or sense of seeing, the power to see something; to look.
classic	/ˈklæsɪk/	Adj.	Of highest class or quality; highly qualitative or rated; a model or guide due to highly established standard.
classical	/ˈklæsɪkl/	Adj.	Traditional or conventional standards

				derived from or based on ancient Greek and Roman models in art or Literature.
coiffeur	/kwaː'fɜː/	N		Hairdresser.
coiffure	/kwaː'fjʊə/	N		Style of hairdressing (particularly adopted by women).
comity	/'kɒmɪtɪ/	N		Intimate relationship which exists between nations or people and creates room for closer ties.
committee	/kə'mɪtɪ/	N		A selected or elected group of people assigned to carry out certain duties within a specified time.
coma	/'kəʊmə/	N		A severe state of unconsciousness.
comer	/'kʌmə/	N		Someone who comes or arrives.
comma	/kɒ'mə/	N		The punctuation mark (,)
complaint	/kəm'pleɪnt/	N		The act of complaining to express annoyance, dissatisfaction, disagreement or grief.
compliant	/kəmpla'ɪənt/	adj.		Willing or accepting to comply with certain order, rules or demands of an authority.
complement	/kɒmplɪment/	N, V		That which gives credibility to something to make it complete or appropriate; to complement
compliment	/'kɒmplɪmənt/	N, V		Expression of good wishes, congratulations or admiration about somebody or something loved.
continual	/kən'tɪnjʊəl/	Adj.		Continuing incessantly or repeatedly, sometime with interruption or short break.
continuous	/kən'tɪnjʊs/	Adj.		Continuing without any break, recess or interruption

co-operate	/kəʊˈɒpəret/	Adj. V	To work in unity or act together in oneness in order to achieve a set goal.
corporate	ˈ/kɔːpərət/		Belonging to a corporation or existing as a member of a unified body of person.
choral	/ˈkɔːrəl/	Adj.	Related or belonging to choir, chorus.
coral	/ˈkɒrəl/	N	Stone-like substance found in the sea bed
corral	/kəˈrɑːl/	N	An enclosure for domestic or wild animal
council	/ˈkaʊnsl/	N	An elected, appointed, or a selected group of persons delegated or assigned to perform certain functions.
counsel	/ˈkaʊnsl/	N, V	Advice, opinion, instruction; to advise.
cancel	/ˈkænsl/	V	Annul, call off, give up or cross out.
course	kɔːs/	N, V	A plan of action that enhances series of movement in space or time, a planned course of study.
curse	/kɜːs/	N	Statement(s) expressing, hate, anger, or dissatisfaction for a wrong-doer, enemy or disapproved person.
cause	/kɔːz/	N, V	Reason, event or person that warrants an event or action to occur; to engender
credible	/kredəbl/	Adj.	(of something) trust-worthy, worthy to be believed.
credulous	/kredjʊələs/	Adj	(of something) quite ready or too willing to believe.
creed	/kriːd/	N	Canon or belief system, formal statement or doctrines of religious belief.
greed	/griːd	N	Avarice, the desire to acquire more.
critic	/krɪtɪk/	N	Person who criticizes; one who assesses a work of art and gives critical judgments

critique	/krɪ'tiːk/	N	or remarks. A critical work of art e.g. essay, review, commentary or remarks written by a critic
croquet	/krəʊkeɪ/	N	An out-door game played on low grass using metal hoop and wooden ball.
croquette	/krəʊket/	N	A kind of palatable meal involving crushed meat, fish, bread, and so on.
crochet	/krəʊʃeɪ/	N, V	A fanciful needle work produced with thread and a small hook; to produce crochet.
crotchet	/krɒtʃɪt/	N	Queer, strange, unreasonable or unusual idea.
cruel	/krʊəl/	Adj.	Wicked, unkind, merciless, and ruthless.
gruel	/'gruːəl/	N	A type of liquid food produced by boiling oat in the milk or water.
crumble	/'krʌmbl/	V	To break into insignificant or negligible parts, or to crush into very small pieces; to decay.
crumple	/'krʌmpl/	V	To crush, collapse or fall down.
grumble	/'grʌmbl/	V	To protest or complain silently or less loudly but angrily to show discontent or discomfort.
cubical	/'kjuːbɪkl/	Adj.	Having, showing or referring to the form of a cube.
cubicle	/'kjuːbɪkl/	N	A small room in the swimming pool for dressing or undressing.
cushion	/'kʊʃn/	N	A small pillow or soft material used in resting one's arm, and so on; a soft lining in the edge of a billiard table.

caution	/ˈkɔːʃn/	N	Admonition or warning given to somebody to avoid danger or to remind of the need to be careful
dead	/ded/	Adj.	(of living things) extinct, no longer alive or existent.
dearth	/dɜːθ/	N	Shortage or scarcity of something essential or useful.
death	/deθ/	N	The noun form of the word "dead" i.e. the end of life.
debauch	/dɪˈbɔːtʃ/	N, V	Lacking virtue; to become vicious, immoral or corrupt.
debouch	/dɪˈbaʊtʃ/	V	To emerge from a narrow place to a larger one
decree	/dɪˈkriː/	N, V	A command, order or legal judgment delivered by a ruler, an authority or a council; to give order.
degree	/dɪˈɡriː/	N	Graduated measurement of angles or temperature; academic title given to scholars in a university.
discreet	/dɪˈskriːt/	Adj.	(of a person's behaviour) – careful, tactful, polite.
discrete	/dɪˈskriːt/	Adj.	Separate, distinct, discontinuous, unique.
desert	/dɪˈzɜːt/	V	To abandon or leave completely, especially at hard time.
	/ˈdezət/	N	Wilderness, barren or waterless land; dry land.
deserts	/dɪˈzɜːts/	N	Something which somebody deserves; plural of desert
dessert	/dɪˈzɜːt/	N	Carefully prepared, palatable fruit, and so on served at the end of a meal.
descent	/dɪˈsent/	Adj.	Ancestry; the act of descending or going down.

decent	/ˈdiːsnt/	Adj.	Respectful, proper, right, modest, acceptable, morally good, suitable.
dissent	/dɪˈsent/	V	To refuse to consent or conform; to disagree
defer	/dɪˈfɜː/	V	To post pone or delay; to give way to something or somebody else.
differ	/ˈdɪfə/	V	To have opposite opinion; to disagree.
deference	/ˈdefərəns/	N	The act of showing respect or approval to somebody or something.
difference	/ˈdɪfrəns/	N	The act of being unlike or different.
desperate	/ˈdespərət/	Adj.	Loss of hope, being in a state of despair, extreme hopelessness resulting in lawlessness.
disparate	/ˈdɪspərət/	Adj.	Distinctive, essentially different from others in terms of nature, type, kind, quality or amount.
decease	/dɪˈziːz/	N, V	Death; to die
disease	/dɪˈziːz/	N, V	An illness often caused by infection; to be ill.
discourse	/ˈdɪskɔːs/	N	A serious conversation, talk, speech, lecture, essay, sermon or dissertation.
discus	/ˈdɪskəs/	N	A heavy round plate of wood, stone or metal used in athletic competition.
discuss	/dɪˈskʌs/	V	To examine, assess or evaluate somebody or something; to talk or argue about something.
disposes	/dɪˈspəʊzəs/	V	Plural form of the verb "dispose".
dispossess	/dɪspəʊˈzəs/	V	To compel somebody (esp. the owner) to give up something; to forcefully take away from the owner.
draught	/drɑːft/	N	A kind of game; depth of water needed to

drought	/draʊt/	N	keep a ship afloat; an air stream flowing through a place. A long period of dry weather causing dryness.
eminent	/ˈemɪnənt/	Adj.	(of a person) famous or prominent; (of quality) outstanding.
imminent	/ˈɪmɪnənt/	Adj.	(of danger or event) likely to occur soon or suddenly.
entrench	/ɪnˈtrentʃ/	V	To dig a deep trench for protection; to establish firmly.
estrange	/ɪˈstreɪndʒ/	V	To cause to become unfriendly; to cause separation.
Economics	/iːkəˈnɒmiks/ /ekəˈnɒmiks/	N	A social science subject studied in school.
Ergonomics	/ɜːgəˈnɒmiks/	N	The study of conditions, environment and the situations that enhance worker's efficiency.
ecstatic	/ɪkˈstætɪk/	Adj.	Causing great joy, excitement or spiritual upliftment.
aesthetic	/iːsˈθetɪk/	Adj.	Concerning or involving the sense of showing appreciation to beauty especially of Arts.
except	/ɪkˈsept/	Prep; V	Apart from; excluding, but, unless.
excerpt	/ˈeksɜːpt/	N	An aspect, fraction, extract or passage taken from a book or any printed material, speech or arts-work.
exert	/ɪgˈzɜːt/	V	To put in, exercise or advance, put force effort.
eternal	/ɪˈtɜːnl/	Adj.	Unending, timeless, ageless, going on for ever.
internal	/ɪnˈtɜːnl/	Adj.	Domestic, within, of or in the inside.

expedient	ɪkˈspiːdɪənt	Adj.	Of something useful or helpful for a purpose but contrary to principle or established convention.
experience	ɪkˈspɪərɪəns	N, V	Knowledge or skill gained through practice or observation to gain knowledge through the influence of surrounding circumstances
faience	/feɪˈɑːns/	N	Earthenware or porcelain made with clay and decorated or ornamental with bright colours.
fiancé	/fiˈɒnseɪ/	N	A man who proposes to marry a lady.
fiancée	/fiˈɒnseɪ/	N	A woman who is engaged in courtship with the fiancé.
fatal	/ˈfeɪtl/	Adj.	Imminent, very dangerous, resulting or ending in death.
vital	/ˈvaɪtl/	Adj.	Essential, important, indispensable, very necessary.
favour	/ˈfeɪvə/	N	An intimate act of encouragement.
fervor	/ˈfɜːvə/	N	Fervency or earnestness.
fission	/ˈfɪʃn/	N	Splitting or division of cells or atoms.
vision	/ˈvɪʒn/	N	Power of fore-seeing, expressing or imagining especially the future.
formally	/ˈfɔːməli/	Adv.	Officially, showing artificiality or convention.
formerly	/ˈfɔːməli/	Adv.	In pervious or earlier times, before now.
freight	/freɪt/	N	Money paid on transportation of goods by water; goods carried in this way.
fright	/fraɪt/	N	Sudden shock resulting from fear or inexperience.

gabble	/ˈgæbl/	V	Gibber, babble, unintelligible sounds produced but not clearly heard.
gable	/ˈgeibl/	N	Three-cornered end of a wall covered by a roof.
garble	/ˈgɑːbl/	V	To select incomplete or unfair proofs from statements; to support false ideas, facts or reports.
gazette	/gəˈzet/	N	An official newspaper or periodical, which contains names of appointees, legal notices or information on promotion of government official.
cassette	/kəˈset/	N	An electronic device containing photographic film or one holding magnetic tape used in radio or cartridge.
glacier	/ˈglæsɪə/	N	Mass of ice formed when snow falls.
glazier	/ˈgleɪzɪə/	N	Person who works on glass.
goggle	/ˈgɒgl/	V	To stare at something with bulging eye; to show surprise.
goggles	/ˈgɒglz/	N	A pair of round spectacles used to protect the eye.
gurgle	/ˈgɜːgl/	N	A sound like that made by water coming out of a bottle with a narrow neck; sounds made by babies when they are happy.
guarantee	/gærənˈtiː/	N, V	An agreement or pledge to fulfill certain conditions; to agree to a written or verbal undertaken.
guaranty	/gærəntɪ/	N	Legal term used for guarantee in legal proceeding.
grate	/greɪt/	N, V	Metal bars or frame that holds coal in a fine place; to rub something against a hard, rough surface.
great	/greɪt/	Adj.	Important, enormous, big, splendid.

grill	/grɪl/	N, V	Something cooked under a great heat; to question severely, closely or continuously.
grille	/grɪl/	N	A framework of metal or wooden bars used to barricade an entrance into a place
grim	/grɪm/	Adj.	Cruel, severe, austere, forbidding.
grime	/graɪm/	N	Thick dirt coating over a surface.
gristle	/'grɪsl/	N	A kind of tough meat.
grizzle	/'grɪzl/	V	To sob quietly and continually; to complain in a self-pitying way.
guide	/gaɪd/	N, V	A leader, something or somebody else; to direct or lead a state of vigilance; to defend or protect; a force.
guard	/gɑːd/	N, V	Officer who watches over somebody or something; to watch.
hackles	/'hækɪz/	N	Long feathers or hairs which stand erect on the back of a cock or other animals in times of danger.
haggles	/'hæglz/	V	Plural form of the verb "haggle", meaning to argue over something e.g. the price of an item.
hangar	/'hæŋə/	N	A building, which houses an aircraft.
hanger	/'hæŋə/	N	A loop or hook devised for hanging clothes
hanker	/hæŋkə/	V	To have a strong wish, craving or desire for something difficult to achieve.
heart	/hɑːt/	N	An internal organ which pumps blood to other parts of the body.
hearth	/hɑːθ/	N	The floor of the fire-place in one's home, and so on.
heath	/hiːθ/	N	An open piece of unlisted land where wild flower or shrubs grow.

infest	/ɪnˈfest/	V	(of animals, insects or birds) to cause trouble, destruction or confusion by appearing in large numbers.
invest	/ɪnˈvest/	V	To put in or give more money or materials for a desired transaction or business.
impale	/ɪmˈpel/	V	To thrust or pierce through with a club or stick to persuade somebody to accept an idea.
impel	/ɪmˈpel/	V	To push forward, drive, force or urge.
ingenious	/ɪnˈdʒiːnjəs/	Adj.	Being clever or skillful in inventing things.
ingenuous	/ɪndʒenjʊəs/	Adj.	Simple, direct, innocent, frank or inexperienced.
invaluable	/ɪnˈvæljʊəbl/	Adj.	Of great or inesteemable value; priceless.
valueless	/ˈvæljʊːlɪs/	Adj	Worthless, without value.
industrious	/ɪnˈdʌstrɪəs/	Adj.	Hardworking; diligent; assiduous.
illustrious	/ɪˈlʌstrɪəs/	Adj	Famous; renowned; greatly distinguished
journalese	/dʒɜːnəˈliːz/	N	The superficial style of journalism ostensibly used to up-grade journalistic art.
journalist	/dʒɜːnlist/	N	A person who specializes in journalism.
kennel	/ˈkenl/	N	Small house where dogs are sheltered, trained and bred.
kernel	/ˈkɜːnl/	N	An eatable part of a nut or any kind of seed contained in a hard shell; the core or an important part of an issue or matter.
colonel	/kɜːnl/	N	A rank in the army
lair	/leə/	N	The dwelling place or den where a wild animal lives or takes refuge
liar	/ˈlaɪə/	N	Person who tells lie.

lack	/læk/	V	Want, need, to be without.
lag	/læg/	N, V	To fall short of, to develop or advance at a slow or abnormal pace.
lark	/laːk/	N	A kind of small bird; a bit of fun or something done to amuse.
ladder	/ˈlædə/	N	A framework of bars or ropes used for ascending or descending heights; something used as a stepping stone.
larder	/ˈlaːdə/	N	A room, cupboard or pantry for storing food items.
later	/ˈleɪtə/	adj; adv	Afterwards, subsequently, comparative degree of later
latter	/ˈlætə/	adj; adv	Recent, modern; the second of two things or people mentioned.
lather	/ˈlɒðə/	N	A white light foam produced by shaking a mixture of soap and water.
leather	/ˈleðə/	N	Tanned or fretted animal skin used in making shoes, bags, belt, and so on.
lessen	/ˈlesn/	V	To reduce or decrease in value, degree or importance.
lesson	/ˈlesn/	N	Knowledge or wisdom acquired through instruction, teaching, learning; an aspect of a subject learned at a time.
liter	/ˈlɪtə/	N	The American version of the word "litre"
litter	/ˈlɪtə/	N, V	Scraps of paper; a kind of bed or strand so onher; to spread or scatter waste paper, and so on. untidily.
literateur	/ˈlɪtrətʃɜː/	N	Person who writes works of Literature.
literature	/ˈlɪtrətʃə/	N	Printed material which are of artistic value or which gives information on a particular subject.
launch	/lɔːntʃ/	V	To cause to begin, to put into action or to

lounge	/laʊndʒ/	N,V	propel e.g. a new boat or aircraft. A comfortable sitting room; to sit; stand or lean in a lazy or relaxed manner.
lunch	/lʌntʃ/	N	Meal eaten at about mid-day.
lunge	/lʌndʒ/	V	To pierce, impel or thrust through with a knife.
lumbar	/ˈlʌmbə/	Adj	Of the loins or located at the lower part of the back.
lumber	/ˈlʌmbə/	N, N	Boards or planks swan from timber; to move in a clumsy or lazy way.
mace	/meɪs/	N	An ancient war club; a king of spice; a kind of ceremonial staff used as insignia of power.
maze	/meɪz/	N	A mental state of confusion or bewilderment; a complicated network of pathways or lines.
mess	/mes/	N, V	A class of military officers taking meals together; disorderly accumulation of items or dirts.
march	/mɑːtʃ/	N	Forceful forward movement with regulated steps as in military parade; the third month of the year.
match	/mætʃ/	N, V	That which has close or sharp resemblance; counterpart; perspective marriage partners; to resemble.
marshal	/ˈmɑːʃl/	N, V	An official in the law court; a military officer of the highest rank; to arrange or organize in systematic order.
martial	/ˈmɑːʃl/	Adj.	That which concerns war or the armed forces.
massage	/ˈmæsɑːʒ/	N, V	The act of robbing, kneading or pressing a persons body with hand to aid circulation, relieve pains or relax the

message	/ˈmesɪdʒ/	N	muscles. Written or spoken information transmitted from one person to another; teaching of important or moral lesson.
massif	/mæˈsiːf/	N	A large range of connected mountains forming one mass
massive	/ˈmæsɪv/	Adj	Enormous, gigantic, bulky, heavy, powerful, unnecessarily large.
mayor	/meə/	. N	A person legally elected by a town council to head a city, town or municipality.
major	/ˈmeɪdʒə/	Adj.; V	Important, main or chief; an army officer with middle rank.
meddler	/ˈmedlə/	N	An intruder; one who insinuates or meddles in other peoples affairs.
medlar	/ˈmedlə/	N	A type of fruit-bearing tree.
manage	/ˈmænɪdʒ/	V	To skillfully influence, direct and control the use of some available resources or ensuing situation.
ménage	/meɪˈnaːʒ/	N	Household i.e. a house and the people living in it.
miler	/ˈmaɪə/	N	Person or horse trained to race a mile.
miller	/ˈmɪlə/	N	One who owns or work in a mile.
missal	/ˈmɪsl/	N	A book of prayers or other religious service used in Roman Catholic church for mass, and so on.
misile	/ˈmɪsaɪl/	N	A projectile or explosive weapon which can be projected or dropped at a target.
measles	/ˈmiːzlz/	N	An infectious disease, especially of children.
metre	/ˈmiːtə/	N	Conventional unit of measurement; specific rhythm in music or poetry.

Word	Pronunciation	Type	Meaning
mitre	/ˈmaːtə/	N	A kind of tall pointed hat worn by priest or Bishop
mood	/muːd/	N	A temporary state of mind indicating one's though; a verbal group which expresses doubt, certainty and so on.
mode	/ˈməʊd/	N	Way, manner or method of doing something; arrangement of statistical data.
motif	/məʊtiːf/	N	A recurrent thematic element on which a work of art, literary work or music is based and developed.
motive	/məʊtɪv/	N; Adj.	Emotion or desire which provides incitement or motivation; cause of or reason for an action.
morning	/ˈmɔːnɪŋ/	N	Dawn, the first or earliest part of the day or earliest part of something.
mourning	/ˈmɔːnɪŋ/	N	Grief especially expresses for the death.
mucous	/ˈmjuːkəs/	Adj.	Of or like mucus; containing mucus.
mucus	/ˈmjuːkəs/	N	Slippery liquid secreted by the mucous membrane.
mulch	/mʌltʃ/	N	Decaying materials used to cover the soil or plants roots to prevent evaporation of moisture.
mulct	/mʌlkt/	N, V	A fine; to fine or forfeit as a penalty for wrong doing.
moral	/ˈmɒrəl/	Adj.	Of or concerning ethical attributes which either portrays human virtues or vices; a lesson derived from such teaching.
morale	/məˈrɒl/	N	A state of mind which shows willingness, confidence, discipline or pride in relation to specific work.
mural	/ˈmjʊərəl/	N	Related to or concerning the wall; decoration placed on the wall.

mystic	/ˈmɪstɪk/	Adj.	Mysterious; of, like or concerning religious mystery or magic.
mystique	/mɪˈstiːk/	Adj.	Descrete cult having mystical or philosophical ideas used as the basis to support an ideology or action.
nautch	/nɔːtʃ/	N	A kind of female Indian dance performed by professional dancing girls in India.
notch	/nɒtʃ/	N	Narrow passage between mountains; a v-shaped cut through something
nudge	/nʌdʒ/	V, N	To touch or push somebody gently in order to gain attention o give a signal; a gentle push.
noble	/ˈnəʊbl/	N	Of distinct quality; high ranking in social class of grand status; praiseworthy in appearance.
nobble	/ˈnɒbl/	V	To weaken somebody or something by druggery or dubious means; to gain somebody's attention by persuading him.
ordinal	/ˈɔːdɪnl/	Adj.	Showing or indicating position or order of number or amount in a set of serial arrangements.
ordinary	/ɔːdɪnrɪ/	Adj.	Usual, common, average.
ordinance	/ɔːdɪnəns/	N	Command or an authoritative order given by a ruler or ruling body.
ordnance	/ˈɔːnəns/	N	Heavy guns; ammunitions, artillery; military supplies.
outcast	/ˈaʊtkɒst/	N	Person forced or ostracized from a home, group, society, and so on.
outcaste	/ˈaʊtkɒst/	N	A person who is no longer a member of his social class (caste) in India.
patten	/ˈpætn/	N	A kind of shoe
pattern	/ˈpætn/	N, V	Excellent example, sample, model; to design a model.

paunch	/pɔːntʃ/	N	Fat stomach, pot belly.
punch	/pʌntʃ/	N, V	To strike or blow with the fist; to poke with a stick; a strike with the fist.
pause	/pɔːz/	N, V	To linger, stop or suspend activity, action or speech for a short time; a musical mark.
pulse	/pʌls/	N, V	A regular throbbing of blood from the blood vessel; seeds growing in pods e.g. beans.
purse	/pɜːs/	N, V	A woman's handbag; a small bag for carrying money.
plague	/pleɪg/	N, V	An epidemic disease which is highly infectious; affliction; pestilence.
plaque	/plaːk/	N	A porcelain or ornamented plate or monument used as a memorial or used for mural decoration.
pledge	/pledʒ/	N, V	Solemn promise or agreement used as security or a guarantee until an obligation is fulfilled.
pouch	/paʊtʃ/	N	A small leather bag for carrying tobacco; gun powder or mail.
porch	/pɔːtʃ/	N	Veranda, balcony; an attachment or roofed platform at an entrance to a house or church.
purge	/ˈpɜːdʒ/	V	To purify, to evacuate or remove; get rid of.
putsch	/pʊtʃ/	N	An abrupt and concealed revolutionary attempt to overthrow a government; insurrection.
pride	/praɪd/	N	Having high opinion of oneself; self respect, dignity or value; deriving satisfaction in oneself.
proud	/praʊd/	Adj.	Arrogant, haughty, disdainful;

			supercilious.
port-hole	/ˈpɔːthəʊl/	N	A small round window or opening on the side of a ship or aircraft.
pot-hole	/ˈpɒthəʊl/	N	A deep hole on the surface of a road caused by traffic, rain, glacier, and so on.
portend	/pɔːˈtend/	V	Be a passage to act or serve as harbinger, omen or warning against an imminent danger.
portent	/ˈpɔːtent/	N	Sign of impending danger or ominous occurrence; an omen.
potent	/ˈpəʊtnt/	Adj.	Powerful, authoritative; strongly effective.
porter	/ˈpɔːtə/	N	A railway attendant, door keep; an employee who carries traveller's luggage.
potter	/ˈpɒtə/	N	Maker of pots or earthenware vessels.
pother	/ˈpɒðə/	N, V	Fuss, worry or anxiety; to trouble.
precedent	/ˈpresɪdənt/	N	An event, decision or instance that involves the use of convention or custom as a model for later action.
president	/ˈprezɪdənt/	N	A head of government, or department; one who presides over a meeting, group of people or an assembly.
précis	/ˈpreɪsiː/	N	An abstract or concise summary of the main points in а speech, talk, article or book.
precise	/prɪˈsaɪs/	Adj.	Exact, correct; specifically stated.
premier	/ˈpremɪə/	N Adj.	Prime minister; supreme; chief; first in position.
premiere	/ˈpremɪə/	N	First public presentation or performance of a cinema film, movie or play.
principal	/ˈprɪnsəpl/	N	Head of an institution, a college or a business department; chief, first or highest in importance.
principle	/ˈprɪnsəpl/	N	Moral rules or ethical judgments used about certain operations.

quest	/kwest/	N	Search for, pursuit of or inquiry into something.
guest	/gest/	N	A visitor to a host; one who lodges in a hotel.
guess	/ges/	V, N	To form an illogical opinion, statement or supposition; to persuade; supposition.
quiet	/'kwaɪət/	adj.	Silent, calm; serene; noiseless.
quit	/kwit/	V	Stop, discontinue, leave or relinquish suddenly or abruptly.
quite	/kwaɪt/	adv.	Entirely, absolutely, completely, utterly or perfectly.
quilt	/kwɪlt/	N	A thick bed-spread or blanket.
guilt	/giːlt/	N	A condition or responsibility resulting from wrong doing.
radical	/'rædɪkl/	N	Fundamental or complete revolutionary changes; of or concerning roof or base; extreme.
radical	/'rædɪkl/	N	The first or embryo root of a young plant.
recent	/'riːsnt/	Adj. Adv.	Modern, fresh, news; occurring not long ago.
resent	/rɪ'zent/	V	Dislike; feel indignant or bitter about somebody or something
renounce	/rɪ'naʊns/	V	To disown, relinquish or give up a claim.
renown	/rɪ'naʊn/	N	Popularity, fame.
riffle	/'rɪfl/	V	To shuffle (e.g. playing cards); to turn over (pages of a book) quickly.
rifle	/'raɪfl/	N	A kind of a gun; artillery piece or firearm.
resole	/'rɪ'səʊl/	V	To put a new sole on a shoe.
rissole	/'rɪsəʊl/	Adj.	A ball of mined meat fried together with other condiments.
roseate	/'rəʊzɪət/	N	Rosy, cheerful; optimistic.
rosette	/'rəʊzət/	N	Any rose-shaped ornament or badge made of silk band or ribbons used for decoration of clothes.
rapture	/'ræptʃə/	N	Ecstasy; excessive delight or extreme happiness, carrying somebody from one

rupture	/ˈrʌptʃə/	V; N	place to another e.g. heaven. Bursting or breaking open; hernia.
safe	/seɪf/	Adj.	Unharmed, protected; secure.
save	/seɪv/	V	To rescue or preserve from danger, harm or hurt.
serve	/sɜːv/	V	To assist, work for or be a servant to somebody or something.
salon	/ˈsælɒn/	N	Guest room; arts gallery or fashion center
saloon	/səˈluːn/	V	A bar, café or restaurant; a social center meant for entertainment or reception for specific purpose.
sauce	/sɔːs/	N, V	Flavourful liquid added to food to make it more palatable; to add flavour to something.
source	/sɔːs/	N	Point of origin; starting point; an author or originator.
souse	/saʊs/	V	To splash water on or immerse in water.
savant	/ˈsævənt/	N	A wise man or learned scholar.
servant	/ˈsɜːvənt/	N	One who serves, works for or assist another (especially a superior authority).
secret	/ˈsiːkrɪt/	N	Hidden knowledge or concealed information.
secrete	/sɪˈkriːt/	V	To produce liquid substance by ejaculation; to conceal.
sleight	/slaɪt/	N	Dexterous trick, cunningness, craftiness; deftness; clever or skillful deception.
slight	/slaɪt/	Adj, V	Meager; negligible in size, degree or amount; frail; to insult or treat rudely.
solid	/ˈsɒlɪd/	Adj, N	Concrete, compact, substantial; not liquid or gas.
sordid	/ˈsɔːdɪd/	Adj.	Shabby, wrand so onhed, contemptible, squalid.
spacious	/ˈspeɪʃəs/	Adj.	Roomy, vast, having or involving enough space.
specious	/ˈspiːʃəs/	Adj.	Plausible, ostensible; deceptive in reality but seemingly true or right in outlook.

Basic English Grammar and Usage

special	/ˈspeʃl/	Adj.	Particular, especial, exceptional, distinctive.
spatial	/ˈspeɪʃl/	Adj.	Involving, pertaining to or concerning space.
splotch	/splɒdʒ/	N	Irregularity, shaped spot, stain, colour or light.
splurge	/splɜːdʒ/	V	Extravagant, luxurious or wasteful spending.
stager	/ˈsteɪdʒə/	N	A person with long years of experience.
stagger	/ˈstægə/	V	Cause to stand, move or walk unsteadily; to lotter.
staff	/stɑːf/	N	A walking stick or supporting pale; workers in an establishment; a pole used as a support
starve	/stɑːv/	V	To (cause to) suffer for want of food or other essential items; to be hungry.
stave	/steɪv/	N, V	Curved stripes of wood used to form the sides of a barrel; to scare with a staff.
staple	/ˈsteɪpl/	V	Major product constantly supplied or produced in a specific region; tin wine used in holding sheets of paper
stable	/ˈsteɪbl/	N, V	Firm, consistent, fixed, maintaining equilibrium.
stationary	/ˈsteɪʃnrɪ/	Adj.	Static, immovable; maintaining a fixed condition or state.
stationery	/ˈsteɪʃənrɪ/	N	Writing materials.
straight	/streɪt/	Adj.; Adv	Erect, upright, honest, accurate; directly.
strait	/streɪt/	Adj.; N	Difficult, narrow, strict as regards moral question; a narrow passage of water joining two sea.
strip	/strɪp/	V	To dismantle, undress completely or plunder.
stripe	/staɪp/	N	A band of colour worn on uniforms to indicate officers ranks or awards; the stroke of a wipe.
study	/ˈstʌdɪ/	N, V	The act of learning or research; a place or subject of study; to learn or investigate.
sturdy	/ˈstɜːdɪ/	Adj.	Strong, vigorous; firm in determination.

suit	/suːt/	N, V	Court proceeding; a set of garment with coat, jacket and trouser or skirt; to match with other items in a group.
suite	/swiːt/	N	Matching set of furniture or objects that belong together; retinue.
suave	/swɒv/	Adj	Outwardly gracious, polite or urbane manner but possibly insincere.
swerve	/swɜːv/	V	To veer, deflect or change direction suddenly.
torch	/tɔːtʃ/	N	Portable flaming or flash light used to illuminate or guide the way through darkness.
touch	/tʌtʃ/	V, N	To nudge; the act of touching.
track	/træk/	N	A passage, rough road, athletic path or route left by foot-prints of person, animals, and so on; course of action.
tract	/trækt/	N	A distributed pamphlet containing concise write-up or short article on moral lesson, political propaganda or social appeal.
tweeter	/ˈtwiːtə/	N	A loud-speaker that produces high-pitched sounds.
twitter	/ˈtwɪtə/	V, N	To titter or talk rapidly; a sound produced by a bird.
urban	/ˈɜːbən/	Adj.	A city in a developed area or town.
urbane	/ɜːˈbeɪn/	Adj.	Elegant; polite; modest.
vast	/vast/	Adj.	Massive, very great in distance, size or amount.
fast	/fast/	Adj.; Adv.	Quick; firmly fixed; quickly.
victual	/ˈvɪtl/	N, V	Provisions; to store or supply a large quantity of food.
virtual	/ˈvɜːtʃʊəl/	Adj.	Existing or being in fact but not openly or generally accepted.
visible	/ˈvɪzəbl/	Adj.	Apparent; conspicuous; that can be clearly

Basic English Grammar and Usage

Word	Pronunciation	POS	Definition
feasible	/ˈfiːzəbl/	Adj.	seen. Possible; practicable.
Wafer	/ˈweɪfə/	N	A kind of biscuit, bread or cake (sometimes used for communion).
waiver	/ˈweɪvə/	N	The act of waving; person who relinquishes a claim, right or privilege.
waver	/ˈweɪvə/	V	To be unsteady; to be indecisive or uncertain.
weather	/ˈweðə/	N	Atmospheric conditions such as rain, wind, snow, sunshine, temperature at a given time or place.
whether	/ˈweðə/	Conj.	If; in either case; if it occurs that…
wether	/ˈweðə/	N	A castrated or gelded male sheep.
wonder	/ˈwʌndə/	N, V	An inexplicable sense of surprise coupled with admiration, perplexity or utter puzzlement.
wander	/ˈwɒndə/	V	To loiter; to move about aimlessly.
wretch	/retʃ/	N	A poor, miserable or unhappy person.
wretch	/retʃ/	V	To vomit or feel like vomiting.
yeast	/jiːst/	N	A prepared agent of fermentation. Containing yeast cells; foam.
gist	/dʒiːst/	N	Main points of an argument or discussion.
yew	/juː/	N	An evergreen tree.
jew	/dʒuː/	N	Somebody from the Hebrew race.
yoke	/jəʊk/	N, V	A wooden bar placed across two oxen to plow or pull a cart; to bear a burden.
joke	/dʒəʊk/	N, V	An act undertaken to cause amusement or ridicule to make jest; to ridicule
zeal	/ziːl/	N	Enthusiasm; eagerness.
seal	/siːl/	N, V	A signet or an emblame used to indicate ownership or originality; to put a seal on something.

Key: TV = Transcribed Version
POS = Part of Speech
N = Noun
V = Verb
Adj = Adjective
Adv = Adverb
Prep = Preposition.

General Remarks on Homophones: It should be noted that the meanings of some homophones are suggested by their pronunciations rather than their spellings as seen in the following cases:

Tear /tɪə/ :	noun – drops of water produced by the eyes
Tear /teə/ :	verb – to rent something into pieces.
Desert /dɪˈzɜːt/ :	verb – to leave or go away, roam, abandon
Desert /ˈdezet/ :	noun – barren, waterless or dry land, wilderness.
Read /riːd/ :	verb – to decipher or study by reading aloud or silently.
Read /red/ :	verb – past tense of "read" /riːd/
Minute /ˈmɪnɪt/:	noun – the record taken at a meeting; the sixtieth part of an hour or day
minute /maɪˈnjuːt/:	adj. – negligible; very small.

It is equally necessary to point out here that a good deal of words in English language derive their meanings mostly from the context in which they occur. Thus, only few words are independently meaningful outside the semantic context in which they are found. So rarely should words be interpreted or used outside its context.

CHAPTER SEVEN

PARTS OF SPEECH

A word may be classified into one of seven functional groups of words acccordng to the work it does in a sentence. These seven groups are: Nouns, Pronouns, Verbs, Adjectives, Adverbs, Prepositons and Conjunctions. The eighth functional group is the one to which belong words used without any grammatical force. Such words are called 'interjections'. Thus, in all, there are eight parts of speech.

Classification of the Parts of Speech.
Parts of speech may be classified into two groups:
1.   Open-System
2.   Close-System

The Open-System Group:
The parts of speech that make up this group include: noun, adjective, adverb and verb. They are open-system because the word entry capacity of each of them is indefinitely possible. New items are constantly being created and no one can make an inventory of all the words in each of them at a given time. No one can limit by any measure the number each may be made up of at a given time. It is not possible, for example to count all the verbs or nouns in English. At the time of counting, new ones may be formed which may not be accounted for.

The use of words in the open-system group provides us with wider possibilities of choices. For instance, the use of a noun (name of a person or thing) as subject of a sentence in the third person singular will give us unending names of males and females and an endless list of animals or other things as possibilities to replace these with. A pronoun can only leave us with three choices:

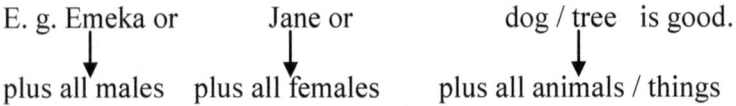

E. g. Emeka or   Jane or   dog / tree is good.

plus all males plus all females plus all animals / things

The possibilities in options for the male gender name, or female gender name, or animal or thing to function as subject of the above sentence is unrestricted or unlimited. However, if one has to replace these possible nouns with a pronoun, there are only three options possible. The sentence will now be:
He or She or It is good.

Closed-system Group

    The closed system group of parts of speech refers to the list of parts of speech in which the set(s) of items found in each member of the list is said to be closed. This means that the set of items cannot normally be extended by creating or forming new ones or additional members. It is not easy to adopt or create another pronoun as an alternative to 'he' for male name in subject positon as it is for nouns. It is easy to arrange all possibilities of pronoun according to person and number. According to Quirk, Greencab, Leech and Svartvik (1979, p.19), it requires no great effort to list all the members of a closed system, and to be reasonably sure that one has made an exhaustive inventory. This is true in the case of relatively so small members like the articles. 'The', 'a' 'an' are the three possibilities of the set of articles. They are reciprocally exclusive. Use of one excludes the use of others.

    A major defining characteristic difference between the open-system group – noun, adjective, adverb and verb and the closed-system group is that it is easy to define a member of open-system group in exclusion of other members. This is not so with the closed-system group – pronon, preposition, conjunction, interjection and articles. For this group, it is much easier to explain the functions of a particular member than one can define its meaning in exclusion of other members in the set. The open-system group are refered to as lexical parts of speech while the closed-system group which are better described in terms of the grammatical functions they perform in an expression are referred to as grammatical or functional parts of speech.

Description of the Parts of Speech
Noun: A noun is the name of a person, an animal, a place, a thing or just a notion. Note that the term 'thing' in the definition also includes the quality, e. g. beauty, honesty, obebience, truth, and so on, an action e. g. theft, murder, and so on.
Example of nouns: Nigeria, Okoro, Ibadan, table, lizard.
Nouns may be further subdivided into other sub-classes such as: common noun, proper noun, count noun, mass noun, concrete or material noun and abstract or immaterial noun.
Common Noun: A common noun is the names of each or many thing (s), or a class of things of the same kind, e. g. bottle, table, knife and chair.
Proper Noun: This is the name of a particular person, animal, place or thing distinguishing it from others of its class e. g. a name of a person, e.g. Okoh; a place, e.g. Abuja; a thing, e.g. Seven Up; or an animal, e.g. Billy (a dog).
Concrete or Material Noun: These are nouns that can be touched, seen or tasted e. g. table, chair, bus.
Abstract or Immaterial Nouns: These are nouns that cannot be touched. They are the names of qualities or states or actions e. g. music, love, truth, flight, and so on. They are therefore the names of abstract or mental conceptions. Abstract nouns are mostly mass nouns.

Countable Nouns: These are nouns whose individual members can be isolated and accounted for, or described e. g. man, house, yam, goat.

Uncountable or Mass Nouns: These are nouns whose individual members are not usually accounted for in isolation. The mass nouns are regarded as uncountable e.g. water, rice, sand, music, crowd, furniture. However, it should be noted that some mass nouns are regarded as countable mass nouns and, therefore, can be pluralized, e.g. arrangements, difficulties, possibilities, and so on.

The figure below graphically presents the major classifications of the nouns in English.

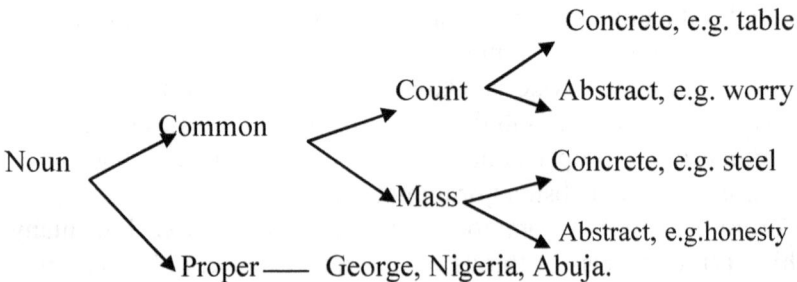

Figure I: Classification of Nouns

There are many nouns with dual class membership – nouns that belong to both classes of count and mass nouns and their meanings differ in the two classes, e. g. the nouns 'experience' and 'talk'.

Consider the words "experience" and "talk" in the following sentences:

(a) EXPERIENCE
(1) The boys had pleasant experiences.
Here the noun "experiences" is a countable noun.
(2) The boys had a great deal of experience.
Here, 'experience' is a mass noun.
(b) TALK

(1) The committee had confidential talks.
Here, 'talks' is a count noun.
(2) I dislike idle talk.
In sentence 2, 'talk' is a mass noun and, therefore, uncountable.

Number in Nouns

There are two terms in English language number system:
(1). The singular: This denotes one
(2). The Plural: This denotes more than one.

There has to be agreement between the subject and a finite verb. The subject that is singular requires a singular verb and a plural subject requires a plural verb. E. g.
1. The boy is playing football.
2. The boy plays football.
3. The hen is chuckling.

In sentence 1, 'the boy' is a singular subject and so takes a singular verb 'is', and so on. If the noun "boy" as subject is plural "boys", then the verb also changes to the plural form, e.g.
The boys are playing football.
Thus singular subject takes singular verb and plural subject takes plural verb. This is what is technically called agreement in English.

Invariable Nouns

Some nouns have no plural maker or some nouns are not plurally marked whether they are in the singular form or in the plural forms. That is, the plural forms do not take 's' or 'es' to denote their plurality. Such nouns are called invariable nouns. The singular category includes common mass nouns e. g. oil, cattle, news, sheep. Also, some concrete mass nouns have no plural markers, e. g. furniture, gold, silver, uranium. Abstract mass nouns have no plural markers. Proper nouns are typically invariable. They only take plural marker in definite circumstances to indicate family e. g. 'Okohs' (the family of people known by the name Okoh). Thus, in this case, Okoh is non-plural and so requires a singular verb. Consider the following sentences.

Basic English Grammar and Usage

1. Okoh is an Engineer.
2. George plays Cricket
3. The National Theatre is a large building.

In these three sentences, the nouns "Okoh", "George" and "The National Theatre" are singular and so take singular verbs respectively.

Variable Nouns

Count nouns are variable nouns, that is, they take the 's' or 'es' suffix to denote their plural forms. They can occur with either singular or plural number, e. g.
Horse – horses; Cat – Cats,
Hen – hens; house – houses; boy – boys.
The summary then is that variable nouns have two forms. The singular and the plural. The singular form denotes one and is unmarked. A vast majority of variable nouns form the regular plural, others form the irregular plurals.

Regular Plurals: These are formed by adding an 's' suffix to the base e. g. 'horse' – base with an 's' suffix added will be 'horses'; boy – boys; cat – cats, and so on.
They are also formed by adding 'es' to the base, e.g. church – churches; match – matches; hero - heroes, and so on.

Spelling of Regular Plural Nouns.
Spelling of reguar plural nouns have certain rules.
Rule 1. Add the 's' suffix to the base including those nouns which end in silence. E. g. horse - horses , marriage – marriages, image – images, language –languages.
Rule 2. Add the 'es' suffix to the base ending in – ch, - s, - sh, - x. The regular plural forms of nouns ending in "–o" have two spellings, -os, -oes. In the following cases, the suffix is: - s, e. g. bamboo – bamboos; kangaroo – kangaroos; quarto – quartos; radio – radios; photo – photos; Romeo – Romeos; kilo – kilos. Examples

of nouns ending in '-o' that has the '-es' suffix include the following: hero – heroes; potato – potatoes; negro – Negroes; echo – echoes; embargo – embargoes; tomato – tomatoes.

Rule 3. When the base ends in '-y' and is preceded by a consoant, then the "y" changes to '-i' and '-es'suffix is added to the base, e.g. country – countries, daisy – daisies, lady – ladies, diary – diaries, lorry – lorries, e. t. c.

However, this rule does not apply to all cases where 'y' occurs. Exceptions are when the base ends in '-y' and is preceded by a vowel, then the plural is formed by adding the '-s' suffix to the base as in Rule 1, e. g. donkey – donkeys, monkey – monkeys, day – days, boy – boys, and so on.

Also, when the base ends in '-y' and the noun is a proper noun, the plural is formed by adding the '-s' suffix. e.g. The Kennedys, the Germanys, the Kimberleys, and so on.

Rule 4. When the base ends in '-f' or in '-fe' in some cases, the '-s' suffix is added e.g. chief – chiefs, - belief – beliefs, chiff – chiffs. In some cases, the '–f' is changed to '–v' and the '–es' suffix is added. E.g. knife – knives, wife – wives, life –lives, leaf – leaves. Some nouns form their plural by doubling the final consonant at the base and adding the '–es' suffix. E.g. fez – fezzes, quiz – quizzes, bus – busses (buses)

Spelling of Irregular Plurals

Irregular plurals are by definition unpredictable plurals, that is, they do not conform to the general rules of how plural forms of nouns are spelt. Their plural forms cannot be inflected from the first sound in the singular of the nouns.
E. g. Stadium – Stadia, medium – media criterion – criteria, ox – oxen, crisis – crises, analysis – analyses, axis – axes, basis – bases emphasis – emphases.

Pronoun

A Pronoun is a word used in the place of a noun, e. g.
Aaron plays cricket.
He plays cricket.
A pronoun can also be used to replace whole noun phrases e. g.
The Headmaster's office is open.
It is open.
The noun phrase (NP), 'The Headmaster's office' is replaced by the pronoun 'it'.
Other examples of pronouns are: she, he, they, you, I, we, us, them, their, this, my, his, her, it, who, whom, whose.

Characteristics of Pronouns.

Many pronouns have certain characteristics that nouns do not have.
1. Pronouns of case contrasts for subject and object cases, e.g.
subject: I, he, we, she, they,
Object: me, him us, her, them.
2. Person distinction e.g. 1st person, 2nd person and 3rd person e. g. I / you / he.
3. Gender contrast – that is masculine and feminine / neuter.
                            he   she   it
Pronouns do not occur with determiners, such as the definite article. Generally, pronouns are subdivided into the following eight sub–classes.

1. Personal Pronouns: These are pronouns representing the person speaking. Such pronouns like "I", "me", "we", "us", and so on, are said to be in the 1st person category. Pronouns which represent the person spoken to are said to be in the second person category e.g. you. The pronouns representing the rest, that is, one or more persons or things mentioned are said to be third person pronouns e.g. 'he", "she", and "it", and for the plural forms, "they" and "them".

2. Possessive Pronouns: They are pronouns used to indicate ownership, e.g. 1st person –mine, ours.
2nd person – yours.
3rd person – his, her, its, theirs.

3. Emphasizing Pronoun – These are pronouns formed by adding the suffix – self (selves) to personal pronouns e.g. himself, herself, itself, themselves, ourselves, myself.
Example of sentences: (i). The Head of State himself was there
(ii). We could not go ourselves.

4. Reflexive Pronoun: It is important to distinguish between the emphatic use of pronouns ending in '–self' and the reflexive use of words. Reflexive pronouns are used as the object or after prepositions and they refer to the same person or thing in the subject, e.g.

      (1) Okoro hurt himself.
      (2) John pinched himself
      (3) We did the work ourselves.
      (4) Jesse passed in all the examinations and gained great honour for himself.

5. Demonstrative Pronouns: These are pronouns that point out the person or thing to which they refer. They are –"these", "that", "this", "those", "such", and "same". E. g.

      (1) This is the boy.
      (2) What is that?
      (3) Who owns those animals?
      (4) That is the man who stole my goat.

6. Interrogative pronouns: As the name implies, these are pronouns used in asking questions e. g. who, what, whose, where.
Examples: (1) Whose is it?
      (2) What did you see?

7. Relative pronouns: They act both as conjuctions joining two clauses together and as pronouns used as subject, object or after a preposition. They are: "who", "whom", "whose", "which", that and "what".They are so called because they relate to a noun or a

pronoun which generally precedes them. The noun or pronoun to which the relative pronoun refers is called the 'antecedent': E.g.
(1) She was the only girl who was dismissed.
(2) The man to whom I gave the letter is the director of the company.

8. Pronouns of Numbers and Amount: They are divided into two: numerical and indefinite pronouns.

(a) *Numerical Pronouns*: These comprise cardinal numbers and ordinal numbers. Example of cardinal numbers are,p.1, 2, 3, 4.
Examples of ordinal numbers are first, second, third, and so on.
Example of sentences with cardinal numbers e.g.
(1) Only two books are in the shelf; I shall remove one.
(2) He purchased three tables, but two were bad.
Examples of sentences with ordinal numbers are:
(1) The first to speak at the meeting was the students union president.
(2) Edewor was the third to pass in First Class Division.

(b) **Indefinite Pronouns**: Indefinite pronouns denote a vague or undefined number or amount. Examples are: any, all, many, each, few, little, much, more, enough, either, someone anybody, everyone, something, and so on.
(1) All attended the matriculation ceremony.
(2) He has enough to eat.
(3) As the visitors arrived each took the place prepared for him.
Note that by using a pronoun, we avoid the repetition of a noun and we mention persons or things without actually naming them.

VERB
  Verbs are parts of speech which express action or state of being which the subject of the sentence performs (in the case of action) or relates (in the case of state of being). E. g.
(1) The messenger swept the office –'swept' expresses the action of the messenger.
(2) The care seems extraordinary.

'Seems' expresses the state of the care.
Verbs are in two categories:
1. The main verb.
2. The auxiliary verb.
1. ***The Main Verb:*** The main verb is also called ***lexical verb***. This is the type of verb which can stand on its own in expressions to show meaning. When the main verb is part of a verb phrase, it is the head of such verb phrase. Examples:
 (1) Sally ate early in the morning.
 (2) Ben has eaten bread.
 In this case, 'ate' is the main verb in sentence 1 while 'has eaten' is a verb phrase and 'ate' heads the phrase with 'has' as an auxiliary verb.
2.***The Auxiliary Verb***: This is usually not regarded as a verb but as a complement element in verb phrases . They are called helping verbs and are usually applied in verb phrases to create tense conditions. However, in a case where there is no obvious main verb, an auxiliary verb functions as the verb. Examples of auxiliary verbs can be seen in the following sentences:
 (1) The students **were** punished (were).
 (2) Sani **is** attending school now (is).
 (3) We **will** see after the meeting (will).
 (4) I **have** a good job. (have – auxiliary as main verb).
 (5) Ojo **is** a Nigerian (is as main verb).
There are two classes of the auxiliary verb: primary and modal auxiliaries.
1.The primary auxilliaries: Three auxiliary verbs are designated as primary auxiliary verb. They are: be, do, have.
Examples: (a) I **am** washing ('am' ⟶ be).
 (b) Ego **did** not wash today (did).
 (c) They **have** worked here before. ('have ⟶ an auxiliary).

2. Modal auxiliaries: Auxiliary verbs are regarded as modal auxiliaries. They function as helping verbs and are combined with main verbs to form verb phrases. The auxiliary verbs are:
will, shall, can, may, could, shoud, might, would, must, need, dare, ought to, used to.

Tense in Verb

Tense is the form of verb that relates the time of an event, action, or state of affairs to the time of speaking or utterance concerning the action, event or state of affairs. On one dimension, tense is also regarded as the grammatical reflection of verbs where by the form which a particular verb assumes relates the time notion in which the action or state of being it expresses is situated.

Taking the moment of speaking as a reference point, a situation may be prior to it. In that case we say that the situation or action happened in the past. The situation obtained in a time reference no longer considered present.

A situation may be simultaneous with the moment of speaking in that case, we say that the situation holds or obtains in the present. That is what is referred to as present tense.

A situation may be subsequent with the moment of speaking, in that case, we say that the situation holds in the future.

From the forgoing we can have defferent time references which are reflected in the verb.

1. A situation simultaneous with the time of speaking – present, Examples:

1. She is 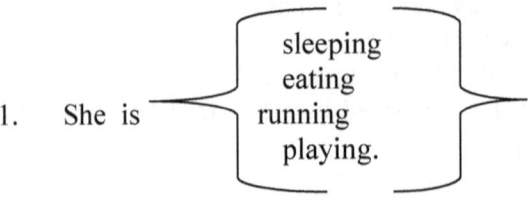 sleeping eating running playing.

2. A situation which obtained or is expressed in a time no longer considered present – past. Examples

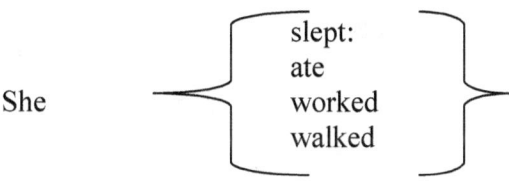

3. A situation that is expressed as obtained at a time that is subsequent to the moment of speaking – future

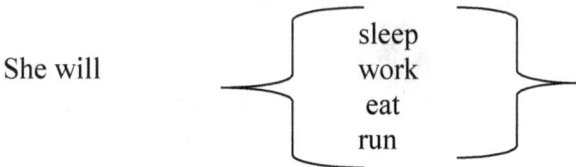

The Different Tense References.
English has two tenses:
1. Present tense
2. Past tense
3. There is a method of expressing a time yet to come called future.

Present tense and past tense have different verb forms which indicate them. There is no form in the verb which shows future tense. Note that there is no obvious future tense in English. Instead, there are a number of ways of denoting future time. The future time is expressed by the use of modal auxiliaries, e. g.

will	would	dare
shall	should	need
may	might	must

can	could	ought
have	has	had
do	did	done

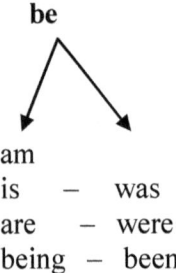

am
is — was
are — were
being — been

Please note the eight forms of the auxiliary verb 'be'.

The Present Tense

The present tense normally refers to the present time. The time in the present may be represented in different time references:

1. *Simple Present Tense*

This is used to signify that an event or action holds or obtains at the moment of speaking. That is, the event or action is simultaneous with the moment of speaking. Example.

(a) John is a university student.
(b) Usman is the president of the students union.
(a) Uche plays in the school's football team.

The events in the above sentences, are happening at the present and go simultaneously with the moment of speaking.

2. *Simple Present with Future Reference*

Future time can also be expressed by the use of the present form. That is, without adding the modal auxiliaries.

Examples:

(1) The plane leaves for Lagos at 7 O'clock.

Notice that the form of the verb "leaves" is in the simple present.

(2) The team departs to Mexico on Tuesday next week.
(3) The University starts her mid-semester examinations on the 16th of December.

It can also be expressed in conditional clauses introduced by if, after, before, unless, as soon as, when. Examples:
(a) The association becomes autonomous *when the bill is passed into law.*
In this sentence, 'when' introduces the conditional clause expressing future time.
(b) She will come as soon as I tell her.
(c) He will carry them if they pay him.

3. *Simple Present with Past Time Reference.* This is used with verbs like 'tell', 'hear', 'write', 'learn'. These verbs are called communicative verbs. They are used to express persistent effect of a past communication in the present. Example:
(a). Mike tells me that you have been in Lagos.
(b).   I hear that Joseph has been abroad.
In the first sentence, the form of the verb is in the present but refers to an event that is happening in the past. This shows an expression of persistent effect.

The Past Tense.
This denotes action or event with time references in the past. As is the case of the present tense, there are different notions of the past tense. These are:

1. *The Simple Past Tense*
This is used to denote what took place at a given time or in a given period before the moment of speaking or present moment. Example:
   (1) I saw him yesterday.
   (2) I saw him last month.
   (3) Okoh played in the team last semester.
   (4) Jane was the President of the Students' Union last session.

There are, however, some exceptional cases in which the past tense is not used to denote an action which took place in the past. One such exceptional case is indirect or reported speeches. The past tense in the reporting verb tends to make the verb of the subordinate clause 'past'.

Example of direct speech – 'you are here'

Reported or indirect speech – 'He said, you were here'. The reporting verb is 'were'.

Attitudinal Past: This is related to the attitude of the speaker rather than to time. The past tense in this is more polite than the present. Examples:

    (1) Present: Do you want to see me now?
         Past: Did you want to see me now?
    (2) Present: I wonder if you can help me.
         Past: I wondered if you could help me.

The tense in the past is preferable to that in the present.

Hypothetical Past: This is used in some subordinate clauses especially the 'if clauses'. Example:

    (1) If I were you, I would not talk.
    (2) If she loved him, she wouldn't do that.

Past Perfect: This means past in the - past, that is, two actions obtained in the past but one of the actions obtained before the other.

Example:

    (1) My mother had come back from the market when I ate my lunch.
    (2) Edward had live in Lagos for five years when I met him.
    (3) I took my bath after my brother came back from the airport.
    (4) Peter had been a student at A. B. U. for two years when I met him.

Expressing Future Time in English *(Future Tense)*

We have mentioned hat there is no obvious form of the verb denoting the future tense. Special ways are adopted to create the future tense.One of the ways of expressing future time is the use of shall + infinitive (An infinitive is that past of a verb that expresses action but has no subject).
Examples: (to go, to be, to lose) plus the 1st person equals future: "shall" plus infinitive with only the 1st person, or
"Will" plus infinitive used with all persons
(1)   I shall try to pass my exams.
(2)   I will try and pass my exams.
(3)   He will be here in half an hour.
(4)   I will be here by tomorrow morning.
(5)   I will do it for you.
(6)   I will carry them for you.
Future time can also be expressed by referring to a statement seen in the past from a position in the future. Example:
(1) She will have graduated by next year.
The whole of the phrase 'will have graduated' refers to the statement seen in the past from a position in te future.
(2) He will have finished the book by next week.
(3) John will have walked fifty kilometers by noon.

Forms of Verb
Regular and Irregular Verbs:
Regular verbs have only four forms.
1.   The base – e. g. call, like, cry, try.
2.   The 'ing' particle – calling, liking, crying, trying.
3.   The 's' form – calls, likes, tries,.
4.   The past '- ed' particle e.g. called, liked cried, tried.
These are regular verbs because we can predict what all the other three forms are, given the base.
Irregular verbs do not have consistent forms as in the case of the regular verbs.go – (went, gone); eat (ate, eaten); cut – (cut, cut). Compare with the regular verbs:

pad   -   padded
pat   -   patted
pass   -   passed
buzz   -   buzzed
work   -   worked
pack   -   packed.

Rules in spelling regular verbs
General Rule: The –'s' form is written as –'s': e. g. look – looks.
The –" ing" form is written as: look – looking.
The – "ed" form is written as: look – looked.
There are four types of exceptions to these rules:
1. The doubling of consonants, e. g.
    bar – barring, that is, it doubles the consonant.
    Beg – begging, begged.
    Permit – permitting, permitted.
    Refer – referring – referred.
    Prefer – preferring, preferred
    Occur – occurring, occurred.
There are expceptions to the rule of doubling of consonants, e. g.
    Enter – entering, entered.
    Visit – visiting, visited
    Dread – dreading, dreaded.
There are other exceptions to the doubling of consonants rule. These occur mainly in British English as distinct from American English with respect to certain other consonants. Examples:

Base	BRE	
signal	- Signalling	– Signalled
program(me)	– programming	– programmed
worship	– worshipping	– worshipped

Base	AME	
travel	- travelling	– traveled traveling, traveled
program	– programing	– programed
worship	– worshiping	– worshiped

Most verbs ending in –p have the regular spelling in both British and American English.

V-base	V-ed₁	V-ed₂
Finite form	**Past Tense**	**Past Participle**
put	put	put
cut	cut	cut
broadcast	broadcast	broadcast
cost	cost	cost
cast	cast	cast
burst	burst	burst
set	set	set
quit	quit	quit
hit	hit	hit
let	let	let
slit	slit	slit
shut	shut	shut
rid	rid	rid
thrust	thrust	thrust
shed	shed	shed
spread	spread	spread
split	split	split

Type two: The three principal parts are different.

V-base	V-ed₁	V-ed₂
arise	arose	arisen
break	broke	broken
choose	chose	chosen
hide	hid	hidden
freeze	froze	frozen
steal	stole	stolen
speak	spoke	spoken

bear	bore	borne
shake	shook	shaken
take	took	taken
give	gave	given
draw	drew	drawn
tread	trod	trodden
lie	laid	lain
do	did	done
drink	drank	drunk
sing	sang	sung
shrink	shrank	shrunk

Type three: The base is the same as past participle: (V-b V-ed$_1$ V) both V and V-ed$_2$ are same and differ from V-ed$_1$.
Example:

V-base	V-ed$_1$	V-ed$_2$
come	came	come
run	ran	run
become	became	become
outrun	outran	outrun

Type four: The simple past is the same as the past participle and they are both different from the base. E.g.

V-base	V-ed$_1$	V-ed$_2$
catch	caught	caught
cleave	cleft	cleft
feed	fed	fed
sell	sold	sold
say	said	said
read	read	read
send	sent	sent
win	won	won
sleep	slept	slept

keep   kept   kept

Type five: The base is equal or same as the past form and they are both different from the past participle.

V-base	**V-ed$_1$**	**V-ed$_2$**
beat	beat	beaten

Aspect of the Verb

An aspect is a category indicating whether an action or state of affairs denoted by the verb action is viewed as completed or in progress, as instantaneous or enduring, as momentary or habitual. In other words, aspect is a way of looking at an event such that the event or action is seen as having the above named phases. These phases could be the beginning, the middle or the end. Event or action may be marked as continuing through time and is referred to as 'progressive aspect'. Progressive aspect is marked by the affix (-ing). Progressive aspect = BE + ING.

Example;

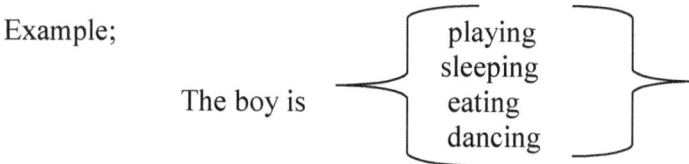

The boy is { playing / sleeping / eating / dancing }

Events may be marked as just beginning in which case the event is conceived of as an **inceptive** aspect, although English does not mark verb directly for the inceptive aspect. It just provides an equivalent construction to indicate this, e.g.
    1. They began walking, singing, eating, running. She started running, eating, and so on.
    2. They began walking at 10 am.
10 am is an inceptive aspect.
    3. They started examinations on Monday.
If the examinations were in progress, then we would talk about **progressive** aspect. Events may be marked as completed and

referred to as the **perfective aspect**. The perfective aspect is marked by affix e.g –ed or en in irregular cases or –d or irregular past tense by an inflection (a change within a word e.g run – ran). Example:

He { played, sang, walked, ran }

(1) The professor types his own letters (iterative aspect).
This is an example of habitual activity, that is, what the professor does all the time.
(2) The professor is typing his own letters (progressive aspect).
(3) I cleaned the window panes that morning (perfective aspect).
(4) I am starting a new job in the company (inceptive aspect).
Note that aspect is the manner in which the verb action is regarded or experienced. It is the comment on or a particular view of the action.

ADJECTIVE

An adjective is a word that is used to qualify or modify a noun or the pronoun. By qualifying, it is meant that an adjective adds something to the meaning of a noun or the pronoun and so limits its application. Example.
- a **happy** ending (happy)
- an **interesting** news (interesting)
- a **beautiful** house (beautiful)

The word 'happy' tells about the nature or type of ending; 'interesting' describes or tells more about the appealing nature of the news and 'beautiful' tells about the appearance of the object 'house'

Classification of Adjectives

1. ***Descriptive Adjectives***: These are those adjectives that describe a person or a thing, e.g. good, beautiful, useful, and so on. for instance:
   1. The builder did a good job.
   2. Beautiful houses are costly to build.
   3. The car was very useful.

2. ***Possessive Adjective:*** Possessive adjectives are 'my' ,'our', 'your', 'its', 'her', 'his', and 'their'. Note that there is a difference between possessive adjectives and possessive pronouns. Examine the following sentences:
   1. This is **mine**.
   2. It is **hers**.   } Pronouns
   3. They said that it was **theirs**.

Compare with:
   (1) This pen is **my** own
   (2) Have you found **your** book?   } Adjectives
   (3) I have seen **their** names

3. ***Emphasizing Adjectives***: examples of emphasizing adjectives are: own and very.
Examples: (1) Her **own** child neglected her.
             (2) The **very** boy insulted him.

4. ***Demonstrative adjectives***: Among these are: these, that, those, this, such, same,
Note that 'the', 'a', 'an', also are demonstrative articles. But, while 'the' is called definite article, 'a', and 'an' are indefinite articles.

5. ***Interrogative adjectives***: Examples are: what and which.
Examples:
   (1) What time did he leave?
   (2) Which car did he buy?

6. ***Relative Adjective***: The words 'what' and 'which' are sometimes used with nouns to introduce relative adjectives e.g

1. He ruled for twelve years during which period Nigeria under went great socio-economic changes.
2. She used what ingredients were best to prepare the dish.

7. *Adjectives of Number or Amount*: These include numerals and indefinite adjectives. The numerals are made up of cardinal numerals e.g. (one, two, three), and ordinal numerals which denote positions in the series, e.g. first place, second place, third place, and so on.

8. *Indefinite adjectives*: Most of the indefinite pronouns may also be used as indefinite adjectives, examples;
1. Such member was allowed to air his view.
2. Some animals are not good for food.

ADVERB

An adverb is a word used to modify or limit the meaning of a verb, an adjective or another adverb. Sometimes adverb qualifies prepositions and conjunctions. Adverbs, however never qualify nouns and pronouns.

Examples of adverbs used to qualify verbs:
1. He writes fast.
2. He responded quickly.

Examples of adverbs used to qualify adjectives are:
1. He became extremely hungry
2. A very old man should retire.

Examples of adverbs used to qualify other adverbs are:
1. He is often fast.
2. He performed fairly boldly.

Note that adverbs generally provide answer to questions, "how, when, where, why and what degree". One of the most common characteristics of the adverb is that it most often ends in the –ly suffix. Also, some adverbs end in –wise suffix, e.g. clockwise, moneywise, otherwise. Many adverbs are derived from adjectives by adding the -ly suffix, e.g. happily, from happy and quickly from quick.

Also note that not all words that end in the –ly suffix are adverbs. Many of such words are adjectives. Although some of such words function both as adjective and adverb.

Examples: (1) He came at an early hour.(adjective)
(2) He was advised to come early.(adverb)
(3) Dickson is sickly.(adjective)

Sickly functions as an adjective qualifying Dickson, although it ends in –ly suffix.

(4) Her manly disposition held her family together.(adjective)
(5) His lively speech entertained us for hours. .(adjective)

Classification of adverbs

Simple Adverbs: simple adverbs denote time, place, number, manner, reason, degree.

Examples of adverbs in the simple class:
(1) Sarah came late.
'late' is an example of an adverb that denotes time.
(2) I have never seen him **so angry.**(adverb of degree)
(3) The soldiers were **walking quickly** there.(adverb of manner)

Interrogative Adverbs: Interrogative adverbs are used in asking questions.

These are: when, where, how, why what, and so on. Examples:
(1) When will they come?
(2) Where did you see her?
(3) How will you go to Lagos?

Relative Adverbs: These are similar to relative pronouns in that they will relate to an antecedent and also join two clauses together.

Examples: (1) I know the place where he stood.
(2) This is the time when people shop for
new articles.

PREPOSITION

A preposition is a word used with a following noun or pronoun to form an adverb phrase or an adjective phrase.

Ordinarily, prepositions function in sentences to relay the relationship between elements in the sentence in terms of position. Prepositions show relationship between two words or phrases in a sentence, and this relationship could be of location, direction or time.eg:

(1) The missing pen was found **under** the table (location).
(2) The bus **to** Oron always runs late on Fridays (direction).
(3) The students studied hard **during** their examination (time).

So when prepositions form adverb or adjective phrases, these phrases relate one notion of position or another.

A phrase is a group of words which does not contain a finite verb but which functions as a single part of speech in a sentence.

A prepositional phrase usually functions as an adjective or an adverb. Examples.

(1) He walked down the stair.
The phrase 'down the stairs, is an adverb phrase qualifying the verb 'walk' it is ruled by the preposition 'down'
(2). A group of soldiers marched through the town.
'through the town' is the adverb phrase qualifying the verb 'marched'
(3) Rogers ran into the room.
'Into the room' is the prepositional phrase or adverb phrase qualifying the verb 'ran'
(4) The driver of the bus alone survived.
The adjective phrase 'of the bus alone survived' is the prepositional phrase qualifying 'driver'
(5) Edward became the president of the students' union government.
The adjective phrase is 'of the students' union government', qualifies the noun 'president'.

Generally, some examples of preposition include: *in, on, through, at, of, into, about, over, across, above, after, against, along, around, before, behind, beneath, under, beside, between, by, down, during, except, for, from, of, since, towards, underneath, up, upon, with*, and so on. Note that most prepositions may also be used as adverbs. The distinguishing feature in these usages is that a preposition is always followed by a noun or a pronoun and the preposition in that case is said to govern the noun or pronoun that follows it.

Examples of words used as adverbs or prepositions:
1. He looked **up**.
2. Ene stayed **behind**.
3. John walked **by** the garden.

'Up', 'behind' and 'by' function both as adverbs and prepositions.

Simple and Complex Prepositions

Most of the common prepositions that occur in English Language are simple prepositions. That is, they consist of one word. Examples: of, at, and so on. There are other prepositions which include more than one word and are called complex prepositions. Examples: as for, as to, away from, into, out of, up to in front of, and so on.

CONJUNCTIONS

A conjunction is a word used to join or connect words or group of words together.

(1) ***Coordinative conjunctions*** are used to join words or phrases or clauses that are co-ordinate, that is, of equal grammatical status and value and therefore independent of one another.

Example:

(1) I waited for him a long time **but** he did not turn up.

'But' is the coordinating conjunction.

Other examples include: still, yet, for, therefore, and, and so on.

(2) *Subordinating Conjunction*: This joins subordinate noun or adverb clause with the main clauses. Some subordinating conjunction are: that, when, since, after, if, unless, how, through, because, as, at, then, that, while.

(3) *Correlative Conjunction*: They are coordinating conjunction used in pairs. Examples, both ...and, either ...or, not only ... but also, and so on.

INTERJECTIONS

An interjection is a word used to express an emotion. Interjections are also called exclamations. Examples; Alas!, Ah!, Hurrah! Interjections are always marked by the exclamation mark '!' Note should be taken when interjection mark denotes a part of speech and when it indicates a sentence.

For example:
(1) Hurrah! , our team has won.
(2) Our team is top!
(3) Alas!, we lost our money.
(4) What a brilliant performance!

'Hurrah!' and 'Alas!' in sentences 1 and 3 are interjections as word or part of speech but the entire sentences where they occur are not exclamatory sentences. On the other hand, sentences 2 and 4 are complete exclamatory expressions and are sentences used to express emotion.

CHAPTER EIGHT

THE ENGLISH WORD STRUCTURE

Linguists generally recognize five units of grammar – morphemes, words, phrases, clauses and sentences (cf Eka, 1994, p.24). These units constitute what is generally referred to in linguistic parlance as grammatical rankscale. On the rankscale, two units – the morpheme and the word – belong to the field of linguistic study usually referred to as morphology.

Morphology: Its Meaning and Content

Morphology is therefore, a branch of linguistic description which is concerned with the study of morphemes and how they are combined to form words. This explains why Tomori (1977, p.21) defines morphology as "the study of the structure of words – the study of the rules governing the formation of words in a language"

Judging from this definition, the morpheme is basically the description of the word structure, and by extension, the grammatical system in any given language. In fact, most linguists define the morpheme in a way that reflects its roles in the entire grammatical system. Tomori (1977,p.16), for instance, defines it as:

> The minimal linguistic element that carries grammatical and/or semantic meaning; it is not further divisible into smaller grammatical components.

Gleason (1969, p.53) and Essien (1990, p.70) describe it as the smallest meaningful unit in the structure of the language. Muir (1972, p.4) views the morpheme as the smallest unit of language on the one hand; and "the smallest unit pertinent to grammatical description on the other". These definitions generally point to the morpheme as that segment of language which is basic to the grammatical and semantic analysis of a given language. These explanations rationalize Gleason's (1969,p.11) remark that the most generally useful method of describing the structure of words is by analysis into morphemes and the description of the ways in which they can be combined.

The morphology of any given languange patterns into two broad branches: lexical and inflectional morphology. Lexical morphology deals with word-formation processes such as derivation and composition or compounding. These can be further subdivided into affixation, back formation, blends, reduplication, suppletion, clipping, conversion and compounding, among others. On the other hand, inflectional morphology marks grammatical (as opposed to lexical) categories such as number, person, gender, tense, mood, voice and aspect (cf Essien, 1990, p.73). We will now examine each of these branches in turn.

Inflectional Morphology

As noted above, inflectional morphology primarily marks paradigmatic relations among grammatical elements – a paradigm being the system of morphemic variations which is correlated with a parallel system of variations in environment (Francis, 1967: 187). This points to what Dinneen (1966: 187) refers to as "covariation" – a functional relation between two things when a change in one is paralleled by a change in the other.

From the explanations cited above, it can be deduced that inflectional morphology is an aspect of grammar which denotes a series of changes in the shape of linguistic forms which matches a series of changes in position (Tomori, 1977: 21). For instance, the paradigms of verb forms will occur in English verbs as conjugated forms thus:

Write	writes	writing	wrote	written
Work	works	working	walked	walked
Put	puts	putting	put	put

Similarly, the noun forms will occur in the following forms:

Man men man's men's
Cat cat's cats'
Stadium stadium's stadia stadia's.

Generally, inflections consider morphological forms as variants of the same word (Francis, 1967:25). Pink and Thomas

(1970: 7) further add that inflection involves a change in form undergone by a word in accordance with a change in its meaning or its relationship with other words in the sentence. Put differently, inflection results from a morphological process which involves changes in the form of a word to indicate strictly grammatical relationships (cf Matthews, 1974: 11,74). In linguistic parlance, the branch of grammar which studies the classification of inflections in languages is referred to as "accidence". Relatively, inflectable forms of words in a language are technically called "allolog" (Pink and Thomas, 1970, 7). In English, inflected forms of word are used to indicate declensions in nouns and pronouns, conjugations in verbs and mutations in adjectives and adverbs.

Inflectional patterns differ from language to language. This is because each language has its own system of structural groupings (cf Fries, 1952: 256; Essien, 1990: 74). For instance, English is both inflectional and analytic, and like Lamberts (1972: 317) has observed, the more inflected a language is, the more items must be in agreement; but the less inflected it is , the less need or opportunity there will be for agreement. English is generally, highly inflected, especially in its verbal, nominal and pronominal forms. This is clear from the patterns of morphemic and morphophonemic variations which are noticeable in English.

Inflectional Morphology

As noted above, inflectional morphology primarily marks paradigmatic relations among grammatical elements – a paradigm being the system of morphemic variations which is correlated with a parallel system of variations in environment (Francis, 1967, p.187). This points to what Dinneen (1966, p.187) refers to as "covariation" – a functional relation between two things when a change in one is paralleled by a change in the other.

From the explanations cited above, it can be deduced that inflectional morphology is an aspect of grammar which denotes a series of changes in the shape of linguistic forms which matches a series of changes in position (Tomori, 1977, p.21). For instance, the paradigms of verb forms will occur in English verbs as conjugated forms thus:

Write	writes	writing	wrote	written
Work	works	working	walked	walked
Put	puts	putting	put	put

Similarly, the noun forms will occur in the following forms:

Man	men	man's	men's
Cat	cat's	cats'	
Stadium	stadium's	stadia	stadia's.

Generally, inflections consider morphological forms as variants of the same word (Francis, 1967, p.25). Pink and Thomas (1970, p.7) further add that inflection involves a change in form undergone by a word in accordance with a change in its meaning or its relationship with other words in the sentence. Put differently, inflection results from a morphological process which involves changes in the form of a word to indicate strictly grammatical relationships (cf Matthews, 1974, p.11, p.74). In linguistic parlance, the branch of grammar which studies the classification of inflections in languages is referred to as "accidence". Relatively, inflectable forms of words in a language are technically called "allolog" (Pink and Thomas, 1970, 7). In English, inflected forms of word are used to indicate declensions in nouns and pronouns, conjugations in verbs and mutations in adjectives and adverbs.

Inflectional patterns differ from language to language. This is because each language has its own system of structural groupings (cf Fries, 1952, p.256; Essien, 1990, p.74). For instance, English is both inflectional and analytic, and like Lamberts (1972, p.317) has observed, the more inflected a language is, the more items must be in agreement; but the less inflected it is, the less need or opportunity there will be for agreement. English is generally, highly inflected, especially in its verbal, nominal and pronominal forms. This is clear from the patterns of morphemic and morphophonemic variations which are noticeable in English.

Variations in Inflectional Morphemes in English

One general view, which linguists admit of language, is its complex nature. The interlacing of linguistic units is a normal occurrence in language. Therefore, there exists a bridge between the phonology and morphology of individual languages. The term ":morphophonemics" is usually used to describe linguistic statements that can be made of the phonemic structure of morphemes and their effect on the grammatical content of any language. In English, for instance, there is a close link between the word structure and its phonological forms. This agrees with Spencer (1991 cited in Udoudom, 1997) that morphology is often enmeshed with phonology. We shall see more of this in our discussion in this section.

In the English language, inflectional morphemes take the form of suffixes. In fact, all grammatical categories in English are indicated through the suffixation process. This is why Francis (1967) remarks that inflectional affixes are all suffixes in English and are capable of marking grammatical functions in the language. Generally, inflectional suffixes are regarded as additive morphemes which function as variants of the same word rather than separate words as in: book – books – book's – books'.

In English, nouns are inflected to mark pluralization and the genetive case; verbs are inflected to mark person, number, tense, mood, voice and aspect while pronouns are inflected for number, gender, case, and person (Pink and Thomas, 1970; Lamberts, 1972; Tomori, 1977).

The plural noun in English basically comprises the base or stem plus the plural morpheme, as in:

girl + s = girls;
cat + s = cats;
rose + s = roses.

Interestingly, a vast majority of English nouns form their plurals by adding an inflectional suffix to the base form. This usually takes various forms as in:
    box – boxes, house – houses, leaf – leaves, knife – knives, lorry – lorries, bus – busses, and so on.

Sometimes plural formation may involve vocalic or intervocalic change in the base form e.g.
    man – men, woman – women, goose – geese, ox – oxen, foot – feet, and so on.

This is referred to as mutation process, which results from a simple vowel alternation, especially from back to front vowel in the plural (Lamberts, 1972). It is mostly explained from the point of view of diachronic linguistics. We are not considering diachronic investigations in a major way in this text.

Some other plural nouns in English occur as zero morphemes (Tomori, 1977; Francis, 1967; Essien 1990). Note that nouns in this category have zero allomorph of the plural morpheme and are classed as irregular, since we cannot predict the sound of the plural on the bases of the singular e.g.
sheep – sheep, cattle – cattle, equipment – equipment.

For the genetive (possessive) case, an "s" suffix is added to the noun base as in: man - man's, men -men's. In written form, both the plural and possessive markers remain invariable. But in speech, there are morphemic variants. This is what we want to examine here.

Tomori (1977) and Eka (1994) observe that the plural and possessive morpheme marker in English {s} is phonologically conditioned and it has three allomorphs (that is variants of the same morpheme), which are /s/, /z/ and /ɪz/ respectively. A fourth is the zero morpheme /Ø/. Several sources explain the occurrence of this morphophonemic phenomena [cf Eka, 1994; Tomori, 1977; Gimson and Cruttenden, 1994; Roach, 1997). Eka (1994), for instance, identifies three sets of the $\{Z\}$ morpheme: $\{Z_1\}$, $\{Z_2\}$, and $\{Z_3\}$. $\{Z_1\}$ morpheme refers to the plural morpheme {s};

{Z_2} morpheme is assigned to the possessive morpheme {'s}, {s'} or {'}; while {Z_3} morpheme reflects the concord or tense morpheme with particular reference to verb inflections (cf Eka, 1994).

With regard to the {Z_1} morpheme, the phenomenon can be explained as follows. When the plural morpheme {s} is attached to any of the words cat, dog and rose, the final suffix is phonologically conditioned to resemble the sound of the immediate environment. Thus, in realizable parlance, the morpheme {s} in cats, dogs and roses will occur in the following sequence: cats /kæts/, dogs /dɒgz/ and roses /'reʊzɪz/ respectively. Therefore, the segments /s/, /z/ and /ɪz/ are allomorphs or variant forms of the plural morpheme {s}. This can be summarily represented thus:

    Cat + s – cats /kæts/   = /s/   ⟶   [s]
    Dog + s – dogs /dɒgz/   = /s/   ⟶   [z]
    Rose + s – roses /'reʊzɪz/ = /s/   ⟶   [ɪz]

The cases of phonological conditioning illustrated above can be explained as follows. First, when the morpheme {s} occurs at the end of a word and is immediately preceded by a voiceless sound other than /s/, then /s/ remains {s}, as in rats, sacks, reaps. Second, if the plural morpheme {s} occurs at the end of a word and is immediately preceded by a voiced sound other than /z, ʒ, dʒ/, the /s/ becomes [z]; as in dogs, boys, balls. Thirdly, if the /s/ plural morpheme is immediately preceded by /z, ʒ, dʒ s, ʃ, tʃ/, then /s/ changes to /ɪz/ as in roses, busses, losses. Based on these analyses, the segments /s/, /z/ and /ɪz/ are said to be allomorphs of the morpheme {s}.

Eka (1994) observes that the fourth allomorph which is not included in the plural morpheme described above belongs to the phonological class usually referred to as zero allomorph, symbolized as /ø/ (cf Essien, 1990). Lamberts (1972) also refers to it as "null" allomorph. Such allomorphs only occur in plural nouns, which have no definite plural markers. Such nouns include aircraft, sheep, cattle, counsel, among others.

The Z_2 morpheme (that is the possessive morpheme {s}) has a distribution similar to the one signified in Z_1 (see Eka, 1994 for a more elaborate treatment on this subject). The major variations that occur are occasioned by orthographic convention vis-à-vis the position of the apostrophe. Thus the possessive morphemes in words like Margaret's /'ma:grets/, men's /menz/ and nurses' /n3:zɪz/ have /s/, /z/ and /ɪz/ as allomorphs of the genetive (possessive)morpheme {s}. Therefore, the phonological conditioning of the possessive morpheme {s} occurs almost in the same way as those explained in (Z_1).

Lexical Morphology

Unlike inflectional morphology, lexical morphology is concerned with word-formation processes comprising two main morphological processes namely: derivation and composition or compounding. These can be further subdivided into derivation. (e.g. affixation- prefixation, infixation, suffixation) and composition or compounding (reduplication, conversion, blends, back-formation), and so on. This implies that lexical morphology is not concerned with merely changing the grammatical forms of a word, but fundamentally deals with the creation of new words from others, such that the new words so created can themselves take on grammatical forms like the one from which they are derived (cf Essien, 1990, p.73). Therefore, lexical morphology results in changes that affect the form-classes of words. This takes place in various ways.

Patterns of English Lexical Morphemes

As noted earlier, one major aspect of lexical morphology is the process of derivation . This comprises affixation in all its forms – prefixation, infixation, and suffixation. Two categories of morphemes can be identified in English in this regard. When morphemes occur independently or can stand on their own without being attached or affixed to some other morphemes for identification and meaning, it is said to be a free morpheme; .but, when they are affixed to the root morpheme, or the stem of a word such that they are capable of performing morphological functions as a result of being attached to the related root, then it is said to be a bound morpheme. In English, in particular, most free morphemes occur before the root of the word while most bound morphemes are affixed after the morphological process referred to as affixation. We will now examine these facts in detail.

Affixation in English.

Affixation is a morphological process which comprises prefixation, infixation, interfixation and suffixation. The forms of word that occur in English, and of course, many other languages of the world, consist of an addition of a basically separate morpheme before an operand, after it or at some determined point within it. This process is called "affixation. The operand comprises the root, the stem or the radical. Roots, stems or radicals are the basis of words. However roots have meaning but radicals have no meaning. In English, morphemes (whether bound or free), which are attached to operands, are called affixes. We can, therefore, define affixes to mean distinct morphemes added to operands (word root, base, stem or radical) to effect changes in the lexical or structural functions of the word referred to as a derivand.

According to Matthews (1974, p.124) affixes are defined by two characteristics: the derivand (the form which result when a process or operation is applied), which consists of the operand (the form that it is applied to) and a new formative which has been added or affixed to it. Affixes are generally subsidiary to the roots, stems or radicals. The roots are frequently longer than the affixes.

Generally, many nouns, pronouns, adverbs and adjectives in English are derived through the process of affixation. As indicated earlier, affixes may take the form of prefixes, infixes, interfixes and suffixes. It is necessary to examine each of these processes more closely.

A prefix is a morpheme added to the root of the word or word base. An interfix is an affix added in between the roots or base of the word. Generally, interfix does not occur in the English language (cf Josiah, 2001). When the affix is added at some point within the root of the word, it is called an infix. But if the morpheme is added after the root or word base, then it is called a suffix. Let us now discuss these in detail.

Prefixation

Prefixation is a morphological process in which prefixes are attached either to the roots, stems or radicals. And prefixes "are affixes or morphemes which precede the roots with which they are most closely associated" (Gleason, 1974, p.59). Most prefixes in English are affixes that function as negative morpheme variants known as allomorph, and they normally occur as free or bond morphemes. The examples in this category include the following:

dis - as in disorganize;
un - as in unstable;
re - as in redistribute.

English prefixes when added to the word base do not generally change the part of speech of the derivand. For instance, the word "dislike" derived from the verb "like" remains a verb and "unholy" derived from "holy" remains an adjective.

Infixation

As stated earlier, an infix is an affix or a morpheme inserted at some point within the root or base of the word. Sometimes, it is used to mark inflectional forms or to show paradigmatic relations. Infixation, therefore, is a process which involves mutation of operands within the stem or word base. Infixation mostly affects inflectional morphology. For instance, one of the ways of forming the past tense of a verb in English is by changing the internal vowel of the verb stem (cf Langacker, 1972, p.65). Thus we have such derivatives as shown below:

Infixes in verbs

Present tense	Past tense	Past participle
Arise	arose	arisen
Drink	drank	drunk
Fall	fell	fallen
Get	got	gotten (got)
Go	went	gone
Ring	rang	rung
Sing	sang	sung

The same situation as explained above can equally be noticed with nominal forms as seen below.

un	- as in unfortunate
ill	- as in ill-treat.
mal	- as in malnourish
mis	- as in misunderstand
im	- as input.

Other prefixes in English can be used to mark increment or addition as it is evident in the following examples:

re	- as in reproduce.
en	- as in enrich
em	- as in empower

Others are used to denote reduction or decrease in value. Here are some examples:

| mini | - as in mini-market |
| quasi | - as in quasi-science |

under   - as in underrate
sub   - as in subdivision
pseudo   - as in pseudo-logic

Generally, most prefixes in English function as free morphemes and are used in building words. Examples include the following:

a-, ab-, abs   - (away from), as in asocial, abdicated, absent.
contra   – (against) as in contraband.
Mis   - (wrong) as in miscalculation
trans   - (across) as in transport
vice   – (instead) as in viceroy, vice chairman

Others can be used to form derivative words between parts of speech. For instance, the noun "asocial" is formed from the adjective "social" and the adjective "undue" is formed from the verb "due"and so on. However, some nominal infixes are inserted intervocalically to mark plural nouns as illustrated below:

Singular	Plural
man	men
woman	women
tooth	teeth
goose	geese
mouse	mice

In each of the inflectional forms above, the infix occur at some determined point within the root, and the internal vowels in each case demonstrate intervocalic change within the word base or stem. In the forms illustrated here, only the existence of the inflectional paradigm permits their combination without recourse to their relevance or structural relationship. Besides the verb forms "go - went – gone" and and the noun forms "mouse" and "mice" constitute to what Francis (1967, p.30) refers to as "suppletion" – that is, "a paradigmatic form having a different stem from the plain form". These distinction are explicable in terms of infixation.

Suffixation

Suffixation is the process of attaching suffixes to either the stems or roots to derive new words. In English, suffixation occurs in most lexical formations (as in happy + ness = happpiness) and in all inflectional formations (e.g. talk- talks- talking - talked), (see Mathews, 1974, p.124)

Most English suffixes do not have their meanings in isolation, but derive them from the root of the word. They can be noun suffix, adverbial suffix, verbal suffix or adjectival suffix respectively. These can variously be illustrated as follows:

Examples of noun suffix:

-an	as in publican
-ance,-ence	as in repentance, existence.
-ician	as in magician, politician
-ness	as in kindness, loneliness
-tion,-sion	as in direction , illustration

Examples or verbal suffix

-ate	as in salivate
-ise,	ize as in memorize, rationalize
-fy,	as in electrify , notify.
-en,	as in enlighten, quicken.

Examples of adverbial suffix.

-ly	as in slowly, mainly
-wise	as in clockwise, moneywise
-wards	as in backwards , westwards
-r, -er, -iest	as in latter ,sooner , earlier,earliest.

Examples of adjectival suffix

-ful	as in doubtful , faithful
-able	as in salebale, countable
-ent	as in referent , different
-ive	as in active, productive
-en	as in respected, painted
-ing	as in revealing, caring
-er,- ier, iest	as in bigger, prettier , prettiest.

Some suffixes in English perform inflectional functions and serve as paradigms of open-ended form-classes, e.g. nouns, pronouns, verbs, adjectives and adverbs, as in.
    boy- boys – boy's – boys' (noun)
    myself – ourselves (pronoun)
    speaks – speaks – speaking (verb)
    dirty – dirtier – dirtiest (adjective)
    late – later – latest (adverb)
According to Matthew (1974, p.124), one major feature of modification is its tendency towards suffixation, which is a characteristic of language. However, the suffix in English does not change the meaning of a word as drastically as does the prefix, but it does change the grammatical functions. For instance, the following suffixes manifest changes in the grammatical functions of the word listed below, without an entire change of meaning.

Verb	Noun	Adjective	adverb
Relate	relation	relative	relatively
Select	selection	selective	selectively

These indicate that suffixes are mostly used for inflectional purposes to show grammatical functions rather than lexical forms.

Compounding
    One other aspect of lexical morphology which English employs is compounding. Sometimes, two or more free morphemes are combined to form words. Compounding, therefore, involves a lexical formation of two or more free morphemes to derive a new formative having related or distinct meaning from the original (cf Josiah, 1997, p.89).
    Many words in English are formed through the process of compounding. Generally, compounding can be used to form:
    a) Compound expressions involving the combination of nouns, prepositions and verbs, e.g.

Well-to-do, son-in-law, man-made, wife-to-be.
b) Compound nouns from separate words, e.g director-general, board-room, fact-finding, subject-matter.
c) Compound words that show fractional parts and compound numbers. E.g. one-third, twenty-one.
d) Non-hyphenated compound expressions composed of an attributive modifier-element that serves as an additive component to a referent in the group, e.g. passport, grandson, aircraft, network, blackboard, grassroot.
e) New compounds that are entirely modifying compounds, e.g. heart-rending, pains-taking, weak-minded, duty-bound.

However, compounding appears to gain acceptability after consistent period of usage, but this sometimes takes a long time depending on the tacit agreement among users.

Blends

Blends involve the "mixture" or merger (blending) of separate words having different meanings to form one word (Josiah,1997, p.89). One group of such words is the one that tends to coalesce two existing words into one. For instance, the word "brunch" is derived by merging the words "breakfast" and "lunch" and it denotes the late morning meal taken between breakfast and lunch. Again, the word "bask" is the blended form of two words. "bang" and "smash" and "geep" is derived from "goat" and "sheep".

Another form of blend involves shortening and merging of two words into one. In this category, we have such words like "cablegram" from "telegram"and "cable", and this denotes a telegram sent by cable., "pulsar" from "pulsating star" and "slum and suburbs is blended into "slurbs", and so on.

Other forms of blend are related to colloquial expressions, such as "disco" from discotheque, mum from "mother" or mummy", "exam" from examination, "poly" from "polytechnic", and so on.

However, some blends are more readily accepted and used within certain linguistic environments than in others. This results from the relevant semantic interpretation associated with such words within the society in which it is being used.

Back–formations

As the name implies, back-formation are words "formed from the back." In this case, new formatives are outrightly created out of an existing one which is deemed to be a derivand (cf Josiah, 1997, p.91; *Encyclopaedia Britannica,Vi,* 1971, p.876). For instance, the word "liaise" is back-formed from "liaison"; "indigene" is back-formed from "indigenous", "bulldoze" is derived from "bulldozer" and "televise" is back-formed from "television".

Generally, there are traces of arbitrariness in back-formations. This agrees with Gleason (1955) that the arbitrariness of language results from accidental choices which are rather irrational or illogical.

Reduplication

Reduplication is a morphological process which entails the repetition of all or part of the radical element of a base morpheme or form. This process is employed to indicate disturbutional plurality, repetition of an action, customary activity, increase in size, added intensity and continuance of an action or event. Most reduplicated forms in English are often repeated forms which do not change the form-classes of words. The following are examples:
    Very very (as in very very good)
    Goody goody
    Pooh pooh.
At other times, the reduplicated forms are partial depending on the parts affected in the radical or stem element. Here are examples:

Chit- chat
Wishy- washy.
However, considering the number of words that fall into this class, it is obvious that reduplication is not a major word-formation process in English.

Conversion
The last morphological process we will like to treat here is conversion. Some two-syllable words in English do serve as different parts of speech depending on the stress position. Particularly, in English, when accentuation determines the form-class to which a word belongs, then the process referred to as conversion has taken place. Examples could be seen in the following words

Nouns	**Verbs**
'import	im'port
'convert	con'vert
'subject	sub'ject
'refuse	re'fuse

The instances above explains the process of conversion whereby the shift in stress position determines the grammatical function of the word. Incidentally, there are limited number of words which fall into this category.

From the morphological processes treated so far, some deductions can be made. First, affixation is a major word-formation process in English. It can result in changes from one part of speech or functional class to another, and can serve different grammatical functions. Secondly, it is clear from our discussions in this section, that while prefixes perform mainly lexical functions, infixes and suffixes mostly perform inflectional functions. By extension, prefixes are basically morphological elements while infixes and suffixes are largely grammatical elements. Interfixes do not constitute a morphological process in English.

Besides, compounding is another major morphological process in English. However, its content is not as enlarged as what obtains in the case of affixes. Thus, English employs the process of affixation more than compounding in its word formation.

Finally, English uses other subsidiary word-formation processes such as blends, back-formation, conversion and reduplication. But, generally, words in these categories are fewer in number than the previous ones. It is, therefore, worthwhile to conclude that the morphology of English language makes use of two main morphological (structural) processes - affixation and composition or compounding and some other subsidiary ones, namely back-formation, suppletion, blend, reduplication and conversion (cf *Encyclopaedia Britannica*, Vi. 1971,p.876).

CHAPTER NINE

THE PHRASE

When two or more words occur in a sentence, they form units of expression. Such units may either be independently meaningful or not meaningful on their own. A phrase takes the form of the latter. It could generally be defined as a group of related words without subject and predicate but which functions as a single unit in the syntax of a sentence (cf Wikipedia, the Free Dictionary). Consider the following examples
All the boys paid their fees.
In this sentence, "all the boys" is a phrase. Some phrases have a head or central element. For example, the word 'boy' in the phrase above. But some phrases may not have any definite head element, particularly those involving generic terms like 'the poor', the rich, the blind, and so on. For instance, in the sentence:
"**The poor** and **the rich** are usually at logger heads", the expressions, 'the poor' and 'the rich' are obviously noun phrases which do not have definite heads.
The followings may be said in describing a phrase:
(1) It is a part of a sentence.
In the example above, 'all the boys' is part of the whole sentence, All the boys paid their fees".
In this case, the phrase is the subject of the sentence.
(2) The phrase has no subject and predicate of its own. e.g.
 Ken and all the students live in the new hostel.
The two phrases underlined here:
'Ken and all the students' and 'in the new hostel', lack subject and predicate.
 (3) The phrase functions as a part of speech in a sentence.
This means that the phrase fits into the same function which a part of speech or a word may perform in a sentence, e.g.
(a) Sani has arrived.

(b) Mr. Sani, the new headmaster, has arrived.
This is like saying one sentence, with two different subjects: 'Sani' and 'the new headmaster'. The phrasal subject, 'the new headmaster' is a noun phrase performing appositive function in this sentence.

(4) The phrase does not make a complete sense or meaning on its own, e.g. the phrase – 'Mr. Sani, the new headmaster' only does not give full sense of an expression until the predicate section of the sentence is added.

Types of Phrases
The following are types of phrases:
1. Noun Phrase (NP)
Noun phrase may further be sub-classified into:
    i. Ordinary noun phrase
    ii. Participial phrase
    iii. Infinitive phrase
    iv. Gerund phrase
2. Verb Phrase (VP)
3. Adjectival Phrase (Adv. P.)
4. Adverbial Phrase (Adv. P.)
5. Prepositional Phrase (P.P.)
6. Absolute Phrase (AP)

Noun Phrase
    The noun phrase (NP) is made up of a noun and its complements and /or modifiers
The complements may be articles, determiners, adjective, gerund, participle, and so on.
e.g. A man
    The man
    The wealthy man
    A moving object
    The wounded lion .
Noun phrase hass two major functions
(1) Functions as the subject of a sentence
    e.g. A man came here.
        The wealthy man bought a car.
In the sentences above, 'A man' and 'The wealthy man' are noun phrases functioning as subject to their respective sentences.
Noun Phrase functions as object of a sentence e.g.
    (1) The wealthy man bought **a car**.
    (2) They stopped **the moving object**.

'a car' and 'the moving object' are the objects of their respective sentences.

Noun Phrases in Apposition
A Noun phrase in apposition comes after a noun or another noun phrase and serves as a complement or a modifier to the noun or noun phrase.

Eg. 1 Mandela, a renoun politician, addressed the rally yesterday.
    2 Mr. Mungo Park, an early explorer, was a determined man.
    3 James, my sister's husband, was invited to the party.

The phrases in apposition in these sentences are:
1. a renoun politician
2. an early explorer
3. my sister's husband.

Classes of the Noun Phrase as Earlier Suggested
(i) the ordinary or traditional noun phrase – This is simple noun phrase made of a noun and its modifier(s) which performs ordinarily as subject or object of a sentence.

Eg. 1 **The wealthy man** lives in our street.
    2 **The Police patrol** team intercepted the deadly gang.

The ordinary or traditional noun phrases in these sentences are:
    1 the wealthy man   – subject   – sentence I
    2 the police patrol team – subject   – sentence 2

(ii) Participial Phrase – This is made up of a particple and a complement. A participle is a verb form used as an adjective to modify a noun. There are two participial forms of the verb:
(a) the present participle with – ing form
(b) the past participle with – ed, or – d, - en, - n, and -t forms.

Examples of – ing participle
        –receding, knowing
Examples of   –ed, -d, -en, -n, and –t participles
        - walked, faded, spaced, taken, grown, taught, sent.

A perfect participle fuses 'having' with the past participle, eg. Having forgotten the story, the reporter made up another one.

A participial phrase may function as noun phrase either as subject or object of the sentence or as sentence modifier.
Participial Phrase as a noun, e.g.
(1) **Scoring good grades** is all he works for in an examination.
(2) **Dried leaves** have less weight than wet ones.
(3) Goats eat **dried leaves**.
In the above sentences, 'scoring good grades' in sentence 1 and "Dried leaves" in sentence 2 function as subjects of the sentences while "dried leaves" in sentence 3 function as objects of the sentences.

Participial Phrase as a Sentence Modifier
E.g. 1. **Seeing the police**, the thieves took to their heels.
    2. **Having seen their teacher**, the students decided to write the exams.
    3. **Caught in the act**, the suspect confessed his previous misdeeds.
The participial phrases functioning as sentence modifiers in the sentences are:
    'seeing the police'   – Sentence 1
    'having seen their teacher' – Sentence 2
    'caught in the act'   – Sentence 3

Infinitive Phrase: - An infinitive Phrase begins with 'to' and is followed by a complement. E.g.: "to perceive", "to behold", "to admire", "to eat", "to read", and so on. An infinitive phrase may function as a subject of a verb or as a modifier.
E.g. 1. **To eat** is very difficult for the patient.
    2. **To err** is human and **to forgive** is divine.
'To eat'; 'to err' and 'to forgive', are used as noun phrases in the above sentences.

Infinitive phrase as modifiers:
    1. We stopped **to admire** the scene.
    2. The water helped **to quench** our thirst.
    3. We always choose language **to suit** an occasion.

In Sentence 1, 'to admire' modifies the verb 'stopped' while 'to quench' modifier the verb 'helped' in Sentence 2.

In sentence 3 'to suit ' is an adjective and modifies the noun 'language'.

Gerund Phrase: A gerund phrase is made up of a gerund and a complement. A gerund is the verb form ending in '- ing' but is used as a noun in a sentence. It is sometimes called verb–noun.

Examples of gerund:
1. **Swimming** is difficult to learn.
2. **Reading** is my hobby.
3. He enjoys **smoking**.

The gerund in these sentences are:
'swimming', 'reading' in sentences 1 and 2 functions as subject of the verb "is" respectively and 'smoking' in sentence 3 particularly functioning as object of the sentence

Examples of gerund phrases:
1. **Swimming across an ocean** is impossible
2. **Reading books** is exciting
3. He enjoys **smoking cigarettes**
4. **Waiting for his turn** is what Joy detests.

Gerund phrases in the above sentences include: -
    'swimming across an ocean'
    'Reading books'
    'smoking cigarrete'
    'waiting for his turn'

Verb Phrase

    A verb phrase is a group that is ruled by a verb with other auxiliary verb (s) as complements. It means that a verb phrase has one main verb with one or more auxiliary verbs as modifiers or complements.The verb phrase functions as a verb in a sentence.

Examples of verb phrases include: "has paid", "is working", "would have finished", "was being questioned". In the following sentences, verb phrases function as verbs:

1. The student **has paid** his fees.
2. The labourer **is working** in the farm.
3. Nkem **would have finished** his duty by evening.
4,. Sanni **was being questioned** on his role in the current demonstration by the workers.
5. The headmaster **may have been offending** teachers without knowing it.

The verb phrase functions as verb and rules the predicate part of the sentence. The head verb of the phrase is the main verb in the sentence and is usually referred to as predicator.

Verbals (Verbal Phrases)

Verbals are words formed from verbs but used as another part of speech. Three verb forms function in the category of verbals. These are:
    1.   Participles;
    2.   Gerunds; and
    3.   Infinitives.

The verb forms that are referred to as verbals are so-called because they are derived from the verb and retain essentially many characteristics of the verbs. A verbal may take any kind of modifier or any kind of complement that a verb may take. Verbals perform verb- like functions but, in addition, a verbal may perform a special role such as functioning as any part of speech at one time or the other. A verbal cannot function as the predicate verb in the sentence because it is an incomplete form of a verb and it cannot make a statement or ask question.

1. ***Participles***: A participle is a verbal which is used as an adjective. A participle is a verb form and has the nature of a verb, therefore it may take modifiers and complements. Participles do not always take modifiers or complements. Very often they are used as pure adjectives and are placed directly before the nouns or words they modify. Sometimes, two particples are used as predicate adjectives after linking verbs.

Examples of participles as adjectives:
1. Julie has a charming outlook – 'charming' modifies 'outlook'
2. Ojo's action was humiliating – 'humiliating' modifies 'action'.
3. She ate the fried egg – 'fried' modifies 'egg'.
4. The boys are watching an interesting movie- 'interesting' modifies 'movie'.

The present participle is the participle that is most commonly used as an adjective. In the following illustrations, the present participles are placed directly before the nouns which they modify. In such cases, these participles are generally used as pure adjectives, e.g.
1. escalating prices;
2. soaring height;
3. dangling modifiers;
4. moving cars;
5. running water;
6. rustling leaves.

Note that when the participle is used as an adjective in other words perform predicative function, it is usually placed before the noun which it modifies. When the participle is used as a predicate adjective, it is found in the predicate part of the sentence and it modifies the subject. E.G.
1. The match was exciting – 'exciting'
2. The story was captivating – 'captivating'.
3. The event was startling – 'startling'.

In the sentences above, the present participles are used as predicate adjectives

Forms of the Participle used as Adjectives:

There are three forms of the participles used commonly as adjectives. They are:
1. The present participle (active voice);
2. The past participle (passive voice);
3. The perfect participle (active voice);

Their past participle does not have an active voice. The present participle usually ends in (-ing). The past participle ends in – ed, - d – t, - n, en. Some irregular verbs have no distinctive verb endings.
The perfect participle is always formed by prefixing or by adding the word 'having' to the past participle, e.g. 'having caught, 'having spoken', 'having walked', 'having drank' and so on.
Examples:
1. The car, **having caught fire**, was completely irretrievable.
2. The president, **having spoken**, sat down gently.
3. All the girls, **having walked for a long distance**, were tired.
4. The participants, **having drank enough wine**, rose up to dance.

***Past participle and the perfect participle*:**
The –ed ending of the past participle is commonly used as an adjective. Examples:
1. The policeman, called to the scene, examined the damaged car.'called' is used to modify the noun 'policeman'.
2. The maltreated and undernourished child was adopted by the nurse. The verbs: 'maltreated' and 'undernourished' are past participles used to modify the noun 'child'.
   1. The children, **frightened by the noise**, fled into their houses. 'frightened' modifies 'children' in the sentence.
   2. The room was littered with plates **left by the guests**. The verb 'left' modifies the noun 'plates' in the sentence.

Adjectival Phrase
An adjectival phrase is a group of words which functions as an adjective in a sentence. Adjectives modify nouns, pronouns or another adjective, e.g.
1. **Fair complexioned** people are easily affected by skin diseases –'fair complexioned' modifies 'people
2. The thief, **very tall and huge**, ran across the other street – 'very tall and huge' post modifies the noun - 'thief'.

3. She painted it red. 'red' is an adjective modifying the pronoun 'it'.
4. Jane put up a constantly moderate performance. 'a constantly moderate' is adjectival and modifies 'performance'.

Adjectival Phrase as Complement of the Subject
The adjectives here specifically complement the subject of the sentences.
E.g. 1. The lady with red handbag is a teacher. 'with red hand bag is an adjectival phrase that complements the subject 'the lady'.
2. The orange is very ripe. 'very ripe' is an adjectival phrase that functions as predicate adjective.
3. Okoh is a man with many talents. 'with many talents' is a complement of the subject 'Okoh'.

Adjectival phrase as complement of the object.
Example:
1. Edet spoke to the boys playing in the field.'playing in the field' complements 'the boys' the object of the sentence.
2. The actress prefers the red coloured dress.
'the red coloured' is an adjectival phrase and modifies the noun'dress', the object of the sentence.

Pre and Post Modification in Adjectival Phrases
Ordinarily, adjectives precede the nouns they modify. e.g.
1. The first London trained Lawyer in our community married a white lady.
'the first London trained' is an adjectival phrase. It follows the noun 'Lawyer' which it modify. It is therefore a case of pre modification.
2. Dresssed in an elegant suit, the chairman addressed the audience 'dressesed in an elegant suit' describes 'the chairman' the subject of the sentence. This is a case of pre-modification because it precedes the noun it modifies or complements. Adjectival phrases may be presented in post modification form. That is, they come after the noun they complement or modify. E.g
1. Edewor, **the Principal of the college**, owns two cars.

2. The car, **very modern and comfortable**, costs less.
3. Sade, **a part-three student of sociology**, won the essay competition.

In the sentences given above, 'the principal of the college' post-modifies the noun 'John' which is the subject of the sentence 1. In like manner, 'very modern and comfortable' post-modifies 'the car' in sentence 2, and 'a part three student of sociology' post-modifies 'Sade'.

Phrases of Other Classes that Function as Modifiers or Adjectival Phrase

1. *The noun phrase as a modifier or complement*: Noun phrase that functions as an adjective or a complement is usually referred to as 'Noun Phrase in apposition'. It is also known as 'dangling modifiers'. The noun phrase in apposition comes in post- modifier position to another noun or noun phrase.

Example:
1. Brown, a professor of medicine, owns two cars.
2. Miss Agbani, the current Miss World, has travelled to London.
3. The new company chairman, a man with great experience and wisdom shall do well.

In the sentences above, the noun phrases that function as complement of nouns or another noun phrase are:
'a professor of medicine' – modifies or complements the noun 'Brown' in sentence 1; 'the current Miss world' - complements the noun phrase 'Miss Agbani' in sentence 2; and 'a man with great experience – complements the nouns phrase and post-modifies 'the new company chairman' in sentence 3.

2. *The Verbal phrase as a complement*: As discussed earlier, verbals are verb forms which perform other functions in sentences. They may take different complements like other verbs and become verbal phrases. A verbal phrase may function as the complement of the noun or a noun phrase. E. g:

1. The children being frightened by the dog ran to their parents.
2. The prisoner attempting to escape injured himself.
3. The judge having thoroughly examined the case acquitted the accused.
4. The maltreated and undernourished child was adopted by the nurse.

The verbal phrases in the above examples are:

'being frightened' – modifies 'the children' in sentence 1;

'attempting to escape' – modifies the prisoner in sentence 2;

'having thoroughly examined' modifies 'the judge' in sentence 3;

'maltreated and undernourished' modifies 'child' in sentence 4.

3. **Prepositional Phrase as a Complement**

Prepositional phrases may function as adjectives in the sentence. They therefore become adjectival phrases because they function as complement or modifiers to noun, pronoun or noun phrases.

Example:
1. The books <u>on the table</u> belong to me
2. The house <u>between the storey building and the garden</u> has been sold.
3. Crops <u>under the shades</u> never do well.

The following are prepositional phrases functioning as complements to nouns or noun phrases:

-'on the table' modifies 'the books in sentence 1.

-'between the storey building and the garden' modifies 'the house in sentence 2.

'under the shadows' modifies 'crops' in sentence 3.

Adverbial Phrase

An adverbial phrase functions as adverb in a sentence. Adverbs modify verbs, expressing *how, when, where* and to *what degree* the action expressed by the verb is performed. There are several other conditions or actions of the verb which the adverbial phrase may explain such as*: how long, how large, how small, how much, to what extent.* Example:
1. He spoke **for a long time**.
2. The goat was sold **at a very cheap price**.
3. They met **at the crossroads**.
4. The dove flies **very swiftly**.
5. The language lecturer came **from Lagos** .

The adverbial phrases in the sentences above include: 'for a long time' in sentence 1 and functions as an adverbial phrase of degree which modifies the verb 'spoke'; 'at a very cheap price' in sentence 2 modifies the verb 'sold'; 'at the crossroads' in sentence 3 modifies the verb ' met'; 'very swiftly' in sentence 4 shows the manner of the verb 'flies'; and 'from Lagos' in sentence 5 shows direction or place and it modifies the verb 'came'.

As may be seen, adverbs generally introduce or explain more about the state or action of the verb. Adverbial phrases do the same. Here are some of the aspects of the action or state of the verb which an adverbial phrase may express in a sentence:

Time: every two days, at half past two
  1. The vendor comes every two days.
  2. The committee meets at half past two.

Place: near the house, at the market square.
  1. The explosives were planted near the house.
  2. All the representatives met at the market square.

Manner: Like mad people, very gently.
  1. The actors dressed like mad people.
  2. Cats move very gently.

Reason: for money, because of hunger.
  1. We dance for money.

2. The labourers could not work <u>because of hunger</u>.

Purpose: to win, in order to.
   1. Our team plays <u>to win</u> and not for entertainment.
   2. We paid <u>in order to</u> be allowed in.

Result: because of, as a result of.
   1. The patient died <u>because</u> of shock from the injury.
   2. John succeeded <u>as a result</u> of hard work.

Condition: If tickled, if offended.
   1. Human beings laugh <u>if tickled.</u>
   2. He refuses to work <u>if offended</u>.

Proportion: more vigorously, to a great extent.
   1. The singer danced <u>more vigorously</u> when the governor arrived.
   2. He worked <u>to a great extent</u>.

Prepositional Phrase

A prepositional phrase is made up of a preposition followed by noun or pronoun. The noun or pronoun may or may not take a modifier. Such noun or pronoun functions as object of the sentence. The prepositional phrase modifies either a noun or pronoun and therefore performs the same function as an adverb or an adjective.

Example:
 1. I will see you <u>after the meeting</u>.
    'after the meeting' is a prepositional phrase but functions as adverbial phrase. It modifies the verb 'see', expressing time.
 2. The staff meeting holds <u>in the conference room</u>.
    'in the conference room' is a prepositional phrase which functions as an adverbial phrase. It modifies the verb 'holds' expressing location or place..
 3. The book <u>with the red cover</u> is lost.
    The prepositional phrase is with the red cover. It modifies the noun 'book' and therefore functions as an adjectival phrase.
 4. The man <u>in green shirt</u> is a soldier.

'In green shirt' has an adjectival function in the sentence. It modifies the noun 'the man'.
5. We believe in God.
'In God' is a complement of the verb 'believe'.
6. The villagers were hostile to us.
'to us' is a compliment of the adjective 'hostile'.

Absolute Phrase

An absolute consist of a noun or pronoun as head followed by a participial phrase.

E.g. (i) *The building having been completed*, the contractor requested for his payment.
(ii) *The information having been delivered to the chief*, the villagers demanded for redress.
(iii) *The exercise being concluded*, the army chief requested for maximum support.

The absolute phrase is usually coordinate in nature and so does not make reference to the subject of the sentence. However, it performs the function of a clause and tends to play the role of a modifying element as could be observed in the sentences presented above.

CHAPTER TEN

THE CLAUSE

A Clause may be defined as a group of related words having both the subject and predicate which is part of a sentence but do not make independent meaning. It also functions as a part of speech in a sentence. The clause is like a sentence because it has a subject and a predicate verb yet it is not a sentence because it is just a part of a complete sentence. Within the sentence in which the clause is a part, the clause does not make a complete sense if it is considered in isolation from the other parts of the sentence (e.g. the subordinate clause).

Example: He read his books, <u>although he did not pass the examination</u>.

'He read his books' is a clause (i.e. main clause) while 'although he did not pass the examination' is another clause (subordinate clause). The two clauses combine to form the sentence given as example above.

Types of Clauses

There are two types of clauses. These are:
1. ***Main Clause*** – also known as independent clause or coordinate clause.
2. ***Subordinate Clause*** – also known as dependent clause.

The Main Clause

A main clause or an independent clause can stand alone as a sentence. The main clause is said to make a complete sense and cannot function as either the subject or the object of the sentence. It does not also function as a complement or modifier.

Examples of main clause:
1. <u>Idris came to the party</u>, although he was late.
2. Until the doctor arrived, <u>no one knew what to do</u>.
3. <u>The students visited their teacher</u> who had been ill.

The main clauses in the sentences above are:

Idri scame to the party – Sentence 1.
No one knew what to do – Sentence 2.
The students visited their teacher – Sentence 3

These parts from their different sentences stand on their own in isolation and make full sense. The difference between a main clause and a sentence is that, for a structure to be known as a main clause, it is part of a larger sentence in which it is the main clause whereas a sentence is a complete expression in its own right. On the other hand, the subordinate clause is a group of words with subject and predicate but cannot stand alone as a sentence. It does not make full sense in isolation, but depends on the main clause for its meaning to be realized. Subordinate clauses are introduced by such words as *who, that, which, also, as if, since, before, after, when, until, how, though, although, eventhough,* and so on. Subordinate clauses may be used in sentences as subjects or objects. They can also function as complements or modifiers.

Examples of subordinate clauses:
1. <u>Idris came to the party</u> although he was late.
2. Until the doctor arrived, <u>no one knew what to do</u>.
3. <u>The students visited their teacher</u> who had been ill.

In Sentence 1, 'although he was late' is a subordinate clause and functions as an adverb modifying 'went'; in sentence 2, 'that I have never had the idea before' is a subordinate clause functioning as a noun and the object of the verb 'admit'. In Sentence 3, 'who arrived late' is a subordinate clause which functions as an adjective and modifies the noun 'student'. In the three sentences above, we have 'an adverbial clause' in sentence 1; 'a noun clause' in sentence 2; and 'an adjectival clause' in sentence 3.

From the preceding, the differences between the main clause and a subordinate clause include:
1. Main clauses are independent and can make full sense; the subordinate clause does not make full meaning on its own; rather it depends on the main clause to make sense.

2. The main clause does not function as subject or object of the sentence. It does not also function as complement or modifier in the sentence. The subordinate clause can form the subject or object of the sentence. It can also function as complement or modifier.

3. Each of the different clauses is introduced or linked in the sentence by specific conjunctions.

The main clause, when linked to another main clause, is introduced by coordinating conjunctions and/or correlative conjunctions such as: coordinating conjunction – *and, but, still, yet, for, therefore*, and so on; correlative conjunctions – (conjunctions used in pairs) both ... and, either ... or, not only ... but also, and so on.

The subordinate clauses are introduced by subordinating conjunctions. These join subordinate noun, adverb and adjective clauses to the main clause. Some words that function as subordinating conjunctions include:

- relative pronouns like: *that, what, which, who, whoever, whom, whose*, and so on.
- subordinating conjunctions like: *although, as after, because, before, if, once, since, that, though, till, unless, until, when, never, where, wherever, while*, and so on.
- Compound subordinating conjunctions like: *as if, as though, soon as, even though, in order that, in that, no matter how, so that* and so on.

Types of Subordinate Clause
There are three types of subordinate or dependent clause.
1. *Noun Clause;*
2. *Adjectival clause;*
3. *Adverbial clause.*

Noun Clause
Noun clauses behave like nouns and are usually introduced by such words as *that, how, why, what, whether* and so on. The

conjunction 'that' is the most frequently used as an indicator of noun clauses. Since noun clauses behave like nouns they perform three basic functions in sentences. These functions are:
1. function of subject of the sentence.
2. function of the object of the sentence.
3. functions of complement in the sentence.

Noun Clause as subject of the sentence
E xample:
1. <u>When you leave</u> is no concern of mine.
'When you leave' is the subject and noun clause.
 2. <u>Whoever pays the price</u> can have the item.
'Whoever pays the price' is a noun clause functioning as subject of the sentence.
 3. <u>That Joy passed</u> is a mystry.
'That Joy passed' is subject and a noun clause.
 4. How Okon made it is a long story.
'How Okon made it' is a noun clause and subject of the sentence.
 5. <u>What the mother bought</u> appears cheap.
'What she bought' is a noun clause and subject of the sentence.
 6. <u>Whether the soldier died</u> is unknown.
The noun clause is 'whether the soldier died' which is the subject of the sentence.

Noun Clause as an Object
    Noun clause functions as object of the sentence.
E. g. 1 The nurse noted <u>that he was drowsy</u>.
   2. The police examined <u>what she carried</u>.
   3. The committee wondered <u>why Segun relinquished his post</u>.
   4. We still wonder <u>whether he lives</u>.
   5. An eye-witness narrated <u>how the robbers were caught</u>.

Noun clauses that function as object in the above sentences are:
    'that he was drowsy' – sentence 1.
    'what she carried' – sentence 2.
    'why Segun relinquished his post' – sentence 3.

'whether he lives' – sentence 4.
'how the robbers were caught' – sentence 5.
Noun Clause As A Complement.
Noun clauses may function as complement in the sentence. Example:
1. The rumours <u>that the president has resigned</u> is false.
2. The news <u>that the student union government</u> has been sacked is true.
3. The story <u>that the ban on partisan politics</u> has been lifted appeared on the Sun Newspapers.

Noun Phrases functioning as complement in the above sentence are:
'that the President has resigned' – complement of the noun 'rumours' – sentence 1.
'that the student union government has been sacked' - complement of the now 'news' – sentence 2.
'that the ban on partisan politics has been lifted' – complement of the noun 'story' – sentence 3.
Note that noun clauses as complements have the following stylistic variations.
1. That the president has resigned is false.
2. That the student union government has been sacked is true.
3. That the ban on partisan politics has been lifted appeared on the Sun Newspapers.
The reverse of the sentences above would be:
1. It is false that the president has resigned.
2. It is true that the student union government has been sacked.
3. It appeared on the Sun Newspaper that the ban on partisan politics has been lifted.

Adjectival or Relative Clause

The Adjectival or Relative clauses perform the functions of adjective and are introduced by the following relative pronouns:

who, whom, whose, which, (these are called continuative relatives) Others are: that (restrictive relative), *when* and *where*. Relative pronouns occur immediately after the antecedents. Relative pronouns such as *who, whom, whose* occur after nouns denoting human beings.

Example: Julie, father, doctor, child, daughter, chairman, boy, sister, uncle and so on.

The relative pronouns *which* and *whose* occur after nouns denoting animals, insects, birds and inanimate things like goat, elephant, tree, table, mercy, hunger, hatred, love and so on. The relative pronoun 'that' occurs after the nouns as for 'which' except proper nouns

Example: It is not used with animate things. 'when' occurs after nouns denoting time as in time, day, hour, minutes, morning, and so on.

Example:
1. This is the time when students have their lunch.
2. This morning is when the exams should begin in all departments.

A relative pronoun 'where' occurs after noun denoting places, as in: place, city, towns, village, house, and so on.

Example:
1. This is the town where the first missionary lived.
2. This is the place where the students burnt the president's effigy.

Restrictive relative clause gives further information to the main sentence. If it is removed, a central idea of the sentence is still retained. It is optional. In spoken English, this begins with such remarks as *by the way, incidentally, you remember*, and so on. They are not normally used in formal language situation.

For example, in the sentence, 'The doctor who cured her is a specialist', the central idea is, 'The doctor is a specialist', therefore the clause, 'who cured her' is a non-restrictive relative clause. The fact that he cured her is incidental to the theme. It can be written as 'The doctor is a specialist'. Incidentally, he cured her.

Any relative clause which accepts this remarks, and which does not add to the central meaning of the sentence, is a non-restrictive relative clause.

There are two distinguishing features of non-restrictive relative clauses.

1. They are not used in formal English.
Example: My brother is gentle. Incidentally, he is a soldier.
They are accepted in spoken English; but, in a formal language, it is written, 'My brother, who is a soldier, is very gentle.
2. A non-restrictive relative clause is marked off from the main sentence by comma.
Example:
 1. I have two friends, who are in London.
 2. My brother, who is a soldier, is very gentle.
 3. My colleaque, who bought the house, is rich.

Note that non-restrictive relative clauses use only the following relative pronouns:
'who', for nouns denoting human beings;
'which', for all other types of nouns. A non-restrictive relative clause does not use the relative pronoun 'that'. In other words, any relative clause introduced by 'that' is a restrictive relative clause. It is the one which identifies the antecedent. It indicates the most important features of the antecedent.

Restrictive relative clauses provide answers to such questions as what?, what for?, who?, so what?, and so on.
Example:
 1. The man, who bought the car, has come.
 2. The Philantropist, who donated the gifts, is very rich.
 3. The politician, who made the speech, is here.
 4. The agent, who sold the car, is rich.
The main sentences regarding the above sentences are:
 1. The man has come.

2. The Philantropist is very rich.
3. The politician is here.
4. The agent is rich.

The sense in the above sentences is very limited in meaning. To avoid questions, we use the restrictive relative clause.

A restrictive relative clause has the following features:

1. It is not separated from the main sentence by commas, e.g. Every Student who needed medical advice was sent to the doctor. The clause 'who needed medical advice' is the relative clause.
   People who live in glass houses should not throw stones.
   'who live in glass houses' is the relative clause.
3. The relative pronoun 'that' is the most frequently used pronoun for restrictive relative clauses.

Adverbial Clause

An Adverbial clause functions as adverb and behaves like adverb. E. g. Okoh was delighted <u>when he found his money intact</u>. The adverbial clause is 'when he found hiss money intact'.

Other examples of adverbial clause:

1. Miss Jane coughed <u>when she took a sip of the wine</u>.
2. The students are now very well behaved <u>so that both men and women are impressed.</u>
3. The audience starred at Alice <u>as if they beheld her for the first time.</u>

The adverbial clauses in the above sentences are: 'when she took a sip of the wine – Sentence 1.

'so that both men and women are impressed' –sentence 2.

'as if they beheld her for the first time. – sentence 3.

An adverbial clause begins with a dependent (subordinating) conjunctions. They expresses a relationship between the clause and the idea denoted by the verb. The adverbial clause like the adverbial phrase or a simple adverb express such notions as time, place, result, reason, condition, and so on.

Types of Adverbial Clauses
Adverbial Clause of Place: where, wherever.
Example: 1. Alice behaves well **wherever she is.**
        2. I know **where Tom lives.**
Adverbial Clause of Time: The subordinate connectives are since, while, when, whenever, after, before, as, and so on.
Example:
    1. The special guest came in **when he left**.
    2. The teacher left **before it started raining**.
    3. Uche went to the market **while it was raining**.
    4. **Whenever I visited John**, his dog barks at me.
    5. **When the storm hit**, the light went off.
Adverbial clauses of time used in the above sentences include:
    1. – 'when he left'
    2. – 'before it started raining'
    3. – 'while it was raining'
    4.– 'whenever I visited John'
    5.– 'when the storm hit'.
Adverbial Clause of Manner uses the connectives such as: as, as if, as though, and so on.
Example:
    1. I wrote the **letter as the manager directed**.
    2. Adam studies **as though his life depends on it**.
    3. He behaves **as if he is intelligent**.
Adverbial Clauses of manner include:
Sentence 1 – 'as the manager directed'.
Sentence 2 – 'as though his life depends on it'.
Sentence 3 – 'as if he is intelligent'.
Adverbial Clause of Cause: uses connectives such as because, as, in as much as, that and so on.
E. g. 1. The patient was glad **that the doctor came**.
    2. Joseph attended the party **because he was invited**.
    3. Third world countries will remain poor **in as much as their resources are not properly managed**.

The adverbial clauses denoting cause are:
Sentence 1 – 'that the doctor came'.
Sentence 2 – 'because he was visited'.
Sentence 3 – 'in as much as their resources are not properly managed'.
Adverbial Clause of Concession: introduced by though, although, even if, e. g.
1. Stella still feels sad **although she was the winner at the contest.**
2. Dan writes badly **although he is in the third year.**
3. I would not have passed in the exams **even if I have studied harder than I did.**
Adverbial Clauses denoting concession are:
Sentence 1 – 'although she was the winner of the context'.
Sentence 2 – 'although he is in the third year'.
Sentence 3 – 'even if I have studied harder than I did'.
Adverbial Clause of Purpose: Often introduced by connectives like that, so that, in order that.
E.g. 1. Oko studied all night **so that he may pass the exams.**
   2. Christ died that we might live.
   3. Wars are fought in order that there may be peace.
Adverbial clauses denoting purpose:
Sentence 1 – so that he may pass the exams.
        2 – that we might live
        3 – in order that there may be peace.
Adverbial Clause of Degree: Usually introduced by connectives like, than, as ... as, so...
E.g. 1. You find the work easier than I do.
   2. Edward ran as fast as he could to escape from the dog.
   3. The road was so muddy that it was rendered impassable.
Adverbial clauses of degree:
1 – 'than I do'
2 – 'as fast as he could'
3 – 'so muddy that it was rendered impassable'.

('that' here signifies a 'resultative 'that')

Adverbial Clause of Result: This is introduced by so, so that and so on.

E. g. 1. The speaker kept repeating himself **so that** the audience could understand.

    2. He worked **so** hard **that** he got 3 As.

Adverbial Clauses denoting Result:

1 – so that the audience could understand
2 – so hard that he got 3 As.

Adverbial clause of Comparison: introduced by connectives like than as …….. as, so …….. as,

E. g. 1. Efe is brighter than Okon is.

    2. Grace is not as clever as her elder brother is.

    3. He looked at me so intensely as to arouse suspicion.

Adverbial clauses denoting comparison:

    1. 'than Okon is'
    2. 'as clever as her elder brothter is'
    3. 'so intensely as to arouse suspocion'.

Adverbial Clause of Condition: introduced by connectives like if, unless, provided that, in case, and so on.

E. g. 1. I shall call the police unless you leave immediately.

    2.The bank gives loans easily provided that you have the collateral.

    3. The criminal was given proper police protection in case other members of the gang came to kill him.

Adverbial clauses denoting condition include:

    1. – unless you leave immediately
    2. – provided that you have the collateral.
    3. – in case other members of the gang came to kill him.

Adverbial clause of Reason: Usually introduced by the connective 'because'.

Note that clauses that express complete thoughts are main clauses and those that do no express complete thoughts are subordinate clauses.

E. g. of adverbial clause of reason:
   1. – He invited him because of his work.
   2. – They agree with him because of what they can gain.
Adverbial clauses denoting reason in the above sentences:
Sentence 1 – 'because of his work'.
          2 – 'because of what they can gain'.

CHAPTER ELEVEN

THE SENTENCE

A sentence may be defined in several ways. It may be described as:
1. an expression that contains one sense unit.
2. a strand so onh of meaningful units of expression.
3. a group of words arranged in a way that makes a complete sense.
4. a unit of utterance that is complete and makes a complete sense.

Two conditions that define a sentence may be pointed at from the definitions given above.

1. A sentence must maintain structural completeness (it is a complete unit or strand so onh of utterance). Some group of words also are units or strand so onhes of utterance but are not sentences because they lack structural completeness.

2. A sentence must make a complete sense. In other words, it should be able to express an idea that is meaningful and quit understandable. The meaning of a sentence therefore should be fully contained in the sentence itself.

Consider the following units in terms of their structural and sense completeness:
1. Early in the morning.
2. When people hurry to their business places.
3. Mr. Ben sleeps.

In the above utterances, it is obvious that numbers 1 and 2 are not complete structurally because they only express some sense of time which in each case is not coordinated either by showing what happens 'early in the morning', or what happens 'when people hurry to their business places'.

The expressions are not complete structurally because each failed to indicate 'who' does 'what', at the time references they express.

In addition to their structural incompleteness, they also lack 'sense completeness'. The full meaning or 'complete sense' cannot be realized from them. Expression 3 is, however, different from 1 and 2. It contains a part that mentions a person (subject) who performs a stated action. So, 'Ben' is one necessary part of the expression and 'sleeps' is another necessary part of the expression. The two combine and form a complete structure because who perform a thing 'Ben' and what he does 'sleeps' are fully represented, the expression makes a complete sense. Therefore, it would be proper to state that expressions 1 and 2 are not sentences but expression 3 is a sentence.

The expressions may be combined at various levels to create completeness.

E. g. 1. Early in the morning Ben sleeps'
    2. When people hurry to their business.
    3. Early in the morning, when people hurry to their business places, Ben sleeps.

Classification of Sentences
The sentence is classified into two types:
1.   according to the functions, and
2.   according to their structures.

Types of Sentence Classification According to Function
This classification criterion distinguishes sentences in accordance with the functions which the different sentences perform when expressed or uttered.

Functional Sentences
There are four basic functional sentence types:

Declarative Sentences:
Declarative Sentences make expressions known as statements, or they state simple facts and conditions
E. g. 1. Nigeria is in West Africa.
    2. We live in Lagos.
    3. Dorothy Edward is a Professor.

4. Today is Tuesday.

Imperative Sentence
Imperative sentences express commands, issues, request, make entreaty or express wishes.
E. g. 1. Suny should do the whole work.
   2. Give me some food.
   3. Nobody should go out of the house today.
   4. Let John come out of the room.

Interrogative Sentence:
Interrogative sentences express questions or simply put, they ask questions.
E. g. 1. Who is the new President of the U.S.A?
   2. What did you do to the boys?

Interrogative sentences have certain features that characterize them:
They are operated by – wh words.
E. g. 1. Where are you going to?
   2. Who is the European best footballer of the year?
   3. How did you know where I live?
   4. When will you go back to Lagos?

Statements may be converted to questions by the use of the auxiliaries and modals as operators.
E. g. 1. Emeka is at home – statement
       Is Emeka at home? – a question
   2. I must go to work - statement
       Must I go to work? – question.
   3. You know where we live. – statement
       Do you know where we live? - question.

Interrogative sentences have an end punctuation mark known as question mark (?). This marks the end of every question and does not require another mark like the full – stop after it to indicate the end of the sentence.

Exclamatory Sentence:
Exclamatory sentences or exclamations are used to express sudden surprise, emotions and excitements.
E. g. 1. What a beautiful car!
    2. Yes, I have made it!
    3. You are wonderful!
The following should be noted about exclamations:
1.   A sentence may not be an exclamation but contains an exclamatory word as part of speech. For example, an expression could be a simple statement or interrogation but may contain an initial exclamatory word.
E. g. in the sentences:
    1. Wow! This house is very beautiful.
    2. What a beautiful house!
In sentence 1, 'wow ' is an exclamatory word but the entire sentence is declarative.
In sentence 2, the entire sentence is a single unit expressing surprise or excitement so it is an exclamatory sentence.
2.   Like the interrogative, the exclamatory sentence has a special punctuations mark (!) at the end of the expression. The exclamatory sentence does not require a full stop after the exclamatory mark to indicate the end of the sentence.

Structural Sentences
    Apart from considering sentences on the bases of the functions they perform, the major grammatical sentence types have the component clauses that make a particular utterance as the ultimate conditions for describing different sentences. Describing sentences according to the clause types that constitute them leads to the realization of different structural sentences as opposed to the functional sentences.
    Structurally, sentences may be described as:

The Simple Sentence
A simple sentence is a sentence that contains only one clause. It is also said to contain one finite verb. In other words, it expresses a single information.

      E.g.   1. Birds fly.
              2. The boys play football.
              3. The headmaster is a kind man
              4. Oranges are sweet.

One remarkable observation about the simple sentence is the absence of conjunction and connectives within its structure.

The Compound Sentence
A compound sentence is composed of two main clauses or two simple sentence joined by co-ordinating conjunction such as; and, but, yet, and so on.

Examples of compound sentences
1. They have eaten the food and there is nothing left.
2. John was an employee here but he has resigned.
3. The rain continued to fall yet the earth remained parched.
4. Janet can go to the market first or she should cook food first.

The combined sections of the compound sentence are said to be of equal rank, or they are independent statements or main clauses.

These two independent or separate statements may be joined to become one compound sentence:
1. The Matron looked at me surprisingly.
2. The Matron asked me what I wanted.

Independent statement 1 and 2 may be joined together to become.

    The Matron looked at me surprisingly and asked me what I wanted.

Note that some sentences as the one above when they are joined together form a compound sentence with the co-ordinating conjunction 'and'.

Complex Sentence

A complex sentence is a sentence that contains one main clause and one or more subordinate clauses. This means that the complex sentence has one central information represented in the main or independent clause. Other notion or notions of information by use of subordinate clauses or dependent clauses.

Examples of Complex Sentences.
1. There was only one car ready for a journey when we got to the motor-park.
2. John will be happy if he sees this results.
3. Alice told a lie because she feared what may befall her.
4. If you arrive early enough, the doctor will attend to you before the crowd gathers.

Sentences 1 and 2 are complex sentences with one main clause and one subordinate clause structures.

Sentences 3 and 4 are complex sentences with one main clause and more than one subordinate clauses.

The difference between a compound sentence and a complex sentence is that there is co-ordination (independent) in the compound sentence whereas there is subordination (dependent) in the complex sentence.

E.g. co-ordination in the compound sentence.

Ade was hungry yet she did not eat anything at the party.

'yet' is a co-ordinating conjunction joining the two independent clauses.

E.g. of subordination in the complex sentence:

I like Janet because she is intelligent.

'because is a subordinating conjunction. So it subordinates the clause it introduces to the main clause 'I like Janet'.

Note that the subordinate clause in a complex sentence is dependent on the main clause for its complete meaning. This is why it is known as dependent clause.

Compound-Complex Sentence

A compound complex sentence has two main clauses and one or more subordinate clauses.

A compound complex sentence may combine one simple sentence and one complex sentence or two complex sentences of different structural formations.

Examples of compound- complex sentences:
1. Aliyu goes to the farm and works until evening whenever it rains.
2. When the police arrived at the scene the mob had dispersed and nobody offered to talk to them because everybody was afraid.
3. If Sally is hungry, she eats whatever is available yet she is very selective of what she eats at ordinary times.
4. When the results were released, the students were happy but some were not.

Multiple Sentence

The multiple sentences contain more than two main clauses. The main clauses are joined together by co-ordinating conjunctions
E.g.
    Jacob likes good foods and he spends a lot of money on that but he does does not earn much money.
1. All the preparations were made in good time and everything was quite in order but the guests never arrived.
2. The employer is very shrewd and pays a peanut but one has to be on a job or would starve to death.

Note that the major differences between the different sentence types lie on the number of main and subordinate clauses they contain and the types of conjunctions that link those component clauses. For instance, the compound complex sentence differs from the multiple sentence because the compound complex sentence contains both main clause and subordinate clause but a multiple sentence contains only main clauses.

The Sentence Structure

The sentence is structured and therefore is composed of different types of sub-structured and grammatical elements. We realize that all the grammatical elements ranging from word, phrase, clause are built into the sentence as the largest grammatical structure that may be realized. It is also worthy of note that the major criterion for defining out sentence types discussed above is the closure types that are found in each sentence type.

In this section, we shall discuss the different methods of assessing the divisions of the sentence and how to identify the different parts that are found in it.

The Subject – Predicate Division

Every sentence may be divided grammatically into two major parts. These parts are the subject and predicate.

The Subject: The subject is that part of a sentence about which something is said in the remaining part of the sentence. It is the part which performs the action or is responsible for the state of being expressed in the verb.

Note that the subject of a sentence may be a person or a thing. Also the subject may be very one word, a phrase or a clause.

The Predicate: The predicate part of the sentence that says something about the subject. It contains the main verb of the sentence. It may also contain other parts of the sentence which add to the information given in the sentence. The predicate like the subject may be one word or group of words.

Examples of sentences showing subject and predicate divisions:

Subject	Predicate
1. Cocks	crow.
2. All mortals	die.
3. Men	grow old.
4. Handsome men	are rich.
5. Aliyu	was born in 1960, the year in which Nigeria gained her independence.
6. All the pensioneers Who reported at Headquarters as directed	were paid.
7. Whoever wins the race	gets one million naira as prize.
8. During the meeting, the chairman	declared that every member shall pay some money.
9. All the congress	Elected Mr. Thomas the new board chairman after much debate

Sentence Elements

In the structure of the sentence, there are some other structural components realized within the sentence, Quirk and Greenbaum (1977, p.16). Most of these elements are within the predicate division of the sentence.

The Predicate in the Sentence

The predicate division has: P (verb, object, compliment and adverbial or adjunct). These can be represented by letters as:

S + P (VOCA)
S – Subject
P – Predicate realized as
V – Verb
O – Object
C – Complement
A – Adverbial or Adjunct

Subject – This has been explained before as that part of the sentence about which something is said in the remaining part of the sentence.

It can be realized by a noun, a noun phrase, a noun clause, a pronoun or any other class of element functioning as a noun.

E.g.   1. John | eats rice.
            S

The Subject as a noun.
       3. The old man | loves little children.
            S -

Subject as a noun phrase
       4. Those men who buy old cars | have come.
                            S

- a noun clause as subject
       5. She | cooks well.
            S

- a pronoun as subject.

       6. Dancing | is a modern profession.
            S

- a gerund as subject
       8. To win a race | is a difficult thing.
                  S

- an infinite phrase as subject

Verb: The verb element is the first item of the predicate part of the sentence. It may be a single word or a phrase (verb phrase)

E.g.   1. Dogs | bark.
            S   V
       2. The students | have eaten food.
                S   V
       3. The Chairman of the occasion | is | here
                              S   V
       4. The cooking | should have finished by now.
                S   V

Note that we did not describe the remaining part of the sentences because we have not yet accounted for the elements they belong to.

Object: The object of the sentence is the element which receives the action of the verb. Another way of putting it is that the object is the element upon which the verb acts. Objects occur in sentences where the verbs are transitive. In that case, the verbs are said to admit an object, that is, the element which receives the action of the verb is present.

There are two types of object elements that may be understood in a sentence depending on the kind of transitivity of the verb.

Basically, a verb a transitive if it admits an object in a sentence.

E.g. 1. Okoh | eats | bread.
          S | V | O   (S V O)

In the above sentence, 'eats' is transitive

A verb is intransitive if it did not admit an object

E.g. Living things eat.
         S   V   (S V)

'Eat' in this example is intransitive, i.e. it does not admit an object.

A verb is mono – transitive if it admits only one object.

E.g. He | wrote | a letter
     S | V | O   (S V O)

The Verb 'wrote' is mono-transitive

A verb on the other hand is di-transitive if it admits two objects

E.g. 1. He | wrote | his wife | a letter
      S | V | O | O   (SVOO)

2. Mary | sent | her friend | some fruits.
     S | V | O | O   (SVOO)

The two types of object are:

1. Direct Object (O_1 or O_d)

2. **Indirect Object** (O_2 or O_{ind})

The object produced when the verb is mono-transitive is a direct object. E. g

The chairman | ate | *Jollof* rice.
      S | V | O_1 (S V O_1)

Di - transitive verbs admit both direct (O_1 or O_{in}) and indirect object (O_2 or O_{ind}.)

    In a sentence, the indirect object usually comes first, followed by the direct object. Another way of identifying the direct and indirect object is to identify the object which received the action expressed in the verb at first hand.

E.g. He | bought | her a | house
     S | V | O | O   (SVO_2O_1)

    Here 'a house' was bought, so 'a house' received the action of the verb first. 'a house' is therefore the direct object O_1 or O_d. The object affected by the action of the verb at secondary level as in the sentence above 'her' is the indirect object, O_2 or O_{ind}.

Further examples: Eze | sent | his parents | some money.
                      S | V | O | O   (SVO_2O_1)

The bank | lent | their customers | huge amount of money
   S | V | O | O   (SVO_2O_1)

Complement: Complement elements have descriptive functions in the sentence. They therefore add more meaning by explaining or describing either the subject or the object of the sentence. Complements are usually items that function as adjectives or noun phrases with descriptive quality. The complement may be a single word or a phrase.

E.g.

1. The soldiers | are | strong.
        S | V | C   (SVC)

2. The Iroko tree | grows | very tall.
        S | V | C   (SVC)

3. John is a famer.
   S   V C   (SVC)

Take note of sentences such as:
   John is a farmer.
   We have seen a farmer.
   A farmer beats John.

In sentence 1, John is a farmer.   (SVC)
'a farmer' is a complement to the subject 'John'.

In sentence 2, We have seen a farmer.
               S   V   O   (SVO)
'a farmer' in the object of the sentence standing for what we have seen.

In sentence 3, A farmer met John. 'A farmer' is the subject of the sentence these explain that a sentence element may be a noun in a particular sentence functioning as either subject or object and an adjective in another expression functioning as a complement.

Complements as adjective element are of two descriptions:

1. **The subject complement** - This is the type of complement which complements the subject of the sentence. It is said to relay information about the subject of the sentence.

E.g.   Sanni is a short man.
        S   V C_s

The answer to the question   seemed very simple.
            S   V C_s

Inyama,   the rich trader   likes oranges.
  S C_s V   O

The complement here is in opposition to the subject of the sentence.

Subject complements are usually introduced by linking verbs. Linking verbs do not express action. They help in making statements by acting as links between the subject and a word in the predicate. They link the subject with nouns or adjectives in the predicate.

e.g. 1. Miss Nancy <u>is</u> a teacher.
2. The herb <u>tastes</u> bitter.
3. The weather <u>was</u> bright.

In these example, 'is' serves as a link between the subject 'miss Nancy' and the complement 'a teacher', 'tastes' links 'bitter' to the subject 'the herb' and 'was' links 'bright' to the subject 'the weather'.

The verb 'BE' is most commonly used as linking verb. Any verbs ending in 'BE' or 'BEEN' is in form of 'BE'.

E.g. shall be, will be, can be, might be, has been, have been, had been, would have been, might have been, and so on.

In addition to 'BE', other verbs serve as linking verbs to subjects and their complements in sentences and their complement in sentences; e.g. seen, appear, look, tasted, become, grow, feel, smell, sound, remain, stay and so on.

E.g. The woman looked very old.

2. Object Complement – The object complements explains or gives more information about the object of the sentence as opposed to the subject complement.

E.g. They | appointed | him | chairman
       S | V | O | C_o -   (SVOC$_o$)
      He | likes | his food | hot
       S | V | O | C_o -   (SVOC$_o$)
      The thieves | painted | the town | red.
          S | V | O | C_o (SVOC$_o$)

The Adverbial Element: The adverbial elements function mainly as adverbs or prepositions. So, basically, adverbs and adverbial phrases are realized as adverbials. Another term used to represent adverbials is adjuncts. According to Quirk et al (1979,p.18) adverbial can be realized :

1. **By adverbial phrases:**
E.g. The police very carefully searched the room
      S   A   V   O

2. The police | searched | the room | very carefully.
     S   V   O   A

2. **By Noun phrase.**
E.g. 1. They | make | him | the chairman | every year.
        S   V   O   C   A

3. **By Prepositional phrase** – that is structure consisting of a noun phrase dominated by a preposition.
e.g, p.1. Alice | studied | at a large university.
        S   V   A

2. Sam | lives | near the stadium.
    S   V   A

4. **By a Clause: finite or non-finite**
1. Far from the large crowd | John | stopped | his car.
          A   S   V   O

2 When he knew he was out of the game, | the former champion | refused to play again
   A   A   S   V

Different structures that may be realized according to the elements discussed so far.

1. The teacher | teaches.   SV
     S   V

2. Yesterday | he | came.   ASV
     A   S V

3. Cats | eats | rats.   SVO
     S   V   O

4. He | was | here.   SVA
     S   V   A

5. Jane | is | a beautiful girl

Basic English Grammar and Usage

	S	V	C$_s$	
6.	He	works	very fast	when he is well fed. SVC$_s$
	S	V	A	A SVAA
7.	He	is	very good	in playing the piano.
	S	V	C	A SVCA

8. The children | saw | Emma | the carpenter.
              S   V   O   C$_o$ SVOC$_o$

9. The artists | danced | beautifully | at the festival
      S   V   A   A   SVAA

10. The manager | paid | them | some money.
       S   V   O$_{ind}$ O$_d$ SVO$_{ind}$O$_d$

11. Yesterday | the students | played | tennis | in the morning.
     A   S   V   O   A   ASVOA

12. When it is possible, | he | goes | to the farm with us.
       A   S V   A   ASVA

13. The Board | appointed | him | the new chairman | at the last congress.
      S   V   O   C$_o$ A   SVOC$_o$A

Voice and Mood in Sentences

Voice: Voice is the grammatical term which is used to tell whether the subject of the sentence is acting or performing the action or is receiving the action expressed by the verb.

When the subject is performing the action it said to be the 'doer'. On the other hand, the subject is the 'receiver' if it is receiving the action expressed by the verb.

E.g.   1. Chuks washed the car.
           Chuks is the doer.
      2. The car was washed by Chuks.

Chuks is not presented as performer of the action in sentence 2.

There are two types of voice:
1. The active voice
2. The passive voice.

Active Voice: when the subject is the doer of the action expressed by the verb it is said to be in active voice.

e.g. Chuks washed the car

"washed" is in active voice.

Passive Voice: When the subject is the receiver of the action, it is in passive voice.

E.g. The car was washed by Chuks

'was washed' expresses a passive voice. or is in passive voice.

Note that Chuks is still in the sentence but it is introduced by a preposition and the verb 'was washed' is said to be in the passive voice because it represents the subject of the sentence as the receiver of the action expressed by the verb.

In other words, the subject is not acting but is Passive and the doer or actor appears in a prepositional phrase.

Note that the verb in passive voice is a simple verb. It is always a verb phrase in the sentence, 'Our books were burnt yesterday' the verb 'were burnt' is in the passive voice. If a verb is in the active voice, the subject is the doer of the action

Voice formulae: Active Voice – Subject = Doer

Passive Voice – Subject = Receiver

An idea in the passive voice cannot be expressed without using an auxiliary or a helping verb and the verb 'to be' in the auxiliary that is used to help form the six tenses of the passive voice

E.g. In the sentences used before:

The car was washed by Chuks and

Our books were burnt yesterday, the verb 'to be' helps the verbs.

The passive voice is formed by combining the verb 'to be' with the past participle of the principal verb. The principal or main verb is

the verb that names the action. In our examples, the verbs 'burnt' and 'washed' are the principal verbs.
Here are more examples:
1. The announcement will be made by the Vice Chancellor.
2. Chairs have been bought for the school by the P.T.A.

The verb in the first sentence is made up of the auxiliary 'will be' and the past participle of the verb 'make' which is made. The verb is used in passive form. The verb in the second sentence 'have been bought' is made up of the auxiliary 'has been' which is the form of the verb 'to be' and the past participle of the verb 'buy' which is 'bought'.

Forms of the Passive Voice.
There are six forms of the passive voice as follows;
(1) Present: 1st person singular: I am calling
              2nd person singular: You are calling
              3rd person singular: He/she/it is calling
              1st person plural: We are calling
              2nd person plural: You are calling
              3rd person plural: They are calling

(2) Past: The examples given above will read thus in past

              1st person singular: I was calling
              2nd person singular: You were calling
              3rd person singular: He/she/it was calling
              1st person plural: We were calling
              2nd person plural: You were calling
              3rd person plural: They were calling

(3) Future: 1st person singular: I shall be calling
              2nd person singular: You will be calling
              3rd person singular: He/she/it will be calling
              1st person plural: We shall be calling

2nd person plural: You will be calling
3rd person plural: They will be calling

(4) Present Perfect
Tense: 1st person singular: I have been calling
          2nd person singular: You have been calling
          3rd person singular: He/she/it has been calling
          1st person plural: We have been calling
          2nd person plural: You have been calling
          3rd person plural: They have been calling.

(5) Past Perfect
Tense: 1st person singular: I had been calling
          2nd person singular: You had been calling
          3rd person singular: He/she/it had been calling
          1st person plural: We had been calling
          2nd person plural: You had been calling
          3rd person plural: They had been calling

(6) Future Perfect
Tense: 1st person singular: I shall have been calling
          2nd person singular: You will have been calling
          3rd person singular: He/she/it will have been calling
          1st person plural: We shall have been calling
          2nd person plural: You will have been calling
          3rd person plural: They will have been calling

Moods in Sentences

Mood is a property of the verb. When the term 'mood' is applied to verb in sentences it means the manner in which the verb expresses the action or state of being of the subject. There are 3 moods on English namely:
  1. The indicative mood

2. The imperative mood
3. The subjunctive mood.

The Indicative Mood
   The indicative mood is used to make statement and ask questions. Most of the commonly used verbs are in the indicative mood
E.g. 1. The secretary wrote a letter. The verb 'wrote is in the indicative mood. The whole of the statement expresses a fact and therefore is in the indicative mood.
   2. Did you see the carpenter?
   The verbs 'did' and 'see' are in the indicative mood. The whole of the expression is a question.

Imperative Mood
Imperative Mood: This is used to express a command or a request. Note that the imperative mood stands only in the present tense of the 2nd person. The subject is always the pronoun 'you' which it seldom expresses.
e.g.   Sit down at once.
       Close the shutters, Bob.
The verbs 'close' and 'sit' are said to be in the imperative mood.

Subjunctive Mood
   Subjunctive mood is used to express a wish or a condition that is contrary to fact. This can be the opposite of the indicative mood. It is used to express something which is contrary to a fact usually expressed by such contrary conditional clauses as 'if' or 'as if'.
E.g. 1. If he were here, I would give him the books.
'Were' in the sentence is in te subjunctive mood.
   2. I wish I were in Jos.
   This is a wish expressed by the verb 'were' and is in the subjunctive mood.

CHAPTER TWELVE

VOCABULARY DEVELOPMENT

Introduction

The word 'vocabulary' generally refers to the total number of words used in a particular language. It can also be used to refer the sum of words used by, or at the command of a particular person or group (Wikipedia, the Free Encyclopedia). Usually, the vocabulary of a language is presented in an orderly manner, mostly in an alphabetical order. It may be presented in the form of word lists, including collocational phrases and idiomatic expressions that are orthographically and semantically relevant to the language in question.

One major framework that seems to depict cyclically, the vocabulary of natural languages is the one that adopts a nine-facet parameter: the written form (orthography), the spoken form (phonology), meaning (reference), concept and reference (semantics), functionality or appropriacy of use (register), lexical relations (collocation), grammatical function (syntax), word structure (morphology) and word associations (synonyms and antonyms) (see Wikipedia, the Free Encyclopedia for a more elaborate treatment of this framework). This source also identifies five types of vocabulary namely:

1. Reading vocabulary – this deals with the total number of words a person can read in a language;
2. Listening vocabulary – the sum of the words in a language that a person can recognize when listening;
3. Speaking vocabulary– all the words a person uses in speech in a particular language;
4. Writing vocabulary– the total number of words used in various forms, ranging from formal to informal writings that are available to a language user; and

5. Focal vocabulary– a specialized set of terms and distinctions that are regularly used by a certain group or an organization, sometimes developed as canonized jargon of an in-group.

However, in this chapter, we will not focus on all these since they form a major content of a more comprehensive study in lexicology. Our interest in this section is to highlight an aspect of the lexicon that deals with word associations namely, synonyms and antonyms.

Synonyms and Antonyms

Synonyms are words with similar or almost similar meanings in a particular language. It is normally used with different implications and associations. On the other hand, antonyms are words that are opposite in meaning to another in the same language.

The knowledge of both synonyms and antonyms is very essential for the development of one's vocabulary. It is apparent that without adequate knowledge of English vocabulary, the choice of appropriate words or alternative expressions would be difficult to make. Therefore, a fair knowledge of synonyms and antonyms of any language is indispensable to ensure effective communication. Each of these semantic concepts will be treated in turn.

Synonyms

The synonyms of English are almost inexhaustible. One of the major reasons why they occur in the language is that during the incursion and subsequent conquest of English territories by divergent hostile groups in England, the languages of such groups were easily adopted by English speakers through commercial activities, social interactions and political leadership (see History of English Language in Chapter 1). The result of these liberal contacts was that many words from various languages of the world which came into English Language began to serve as alternative expressions to already existing English words. Moreover, according to Brook (1958, p.29), one "possible explanation of linguistic resemblances is that the two languages concerned have developed from common source" and exhibit characteristics of a common ancestor. Such words came to be used side by side with English vocabulary and this resulted in two or more words having similar or almost similar meaning. For instance, to mark human environment, English uses words like town, borough, hall, house, room, bower and home while French uses words like city, village, court, palace, manor, mansion, residence and domicile.

This chapter will, therefore, treat a few synonyms in English so as to induce the reader to enlarge his/her vocabulary, having known the background of English synonyms as stated above.

Words	**Synonyms**
Accuse	indict, charge, convict, impeach, arraign, incriminate, question.
adjust:	adapt, accommodate, fit, conform, reconcile, compromise.
adulterated:	Polluted, stained, tarnished, faked, tainted, decadent, contaminated, dirty, sullied, grimy, impure.
advise:	counsel, advocate, recommend, suggest, prescribe.
affirm:	confirm, establish, allege, aver, maintain, vow, assert, testify, declare, asseverate, corroborate, uphold, proclaim.
agree:	concur, correspond, jibe, tally, admit, coincide, consent, acquiesce, assent, subscribe, accept, connive, acknowledge, endorse, approve.
alter:	change, convert, transform, modify, transfigure, translate, transmogrify.

anarchy:`	commotion, imbroglio, trouble, fiasco, chaos, skirmish, disorder, atrocity, rumpus, uproar, insurrection, putsch, clutter, confusion, violence, pother.
argue:	debate, discuss, dispute, reason.
arise:	emerge, emanate, originate, result, stem, issue
arouse:	stir, stimulate, excite, incite, propel, goad, prod, impel, galvanize, motivate, urge, rouse, coax, poise, instigate, provoke, foment, titillate, persuade, cajole, jolt, spur.
arrange:	organize, order, classify, sort, marshal.
artificial:	fake, spurious, imaginary, forged, false, counterfeit, shoddy, apocryphal, illusory, hypocritical, invented, unreal, unnatural, deceptive.
ask:	order, request, demand, require.
assume:	guess, suppose, imagine, conjecture, surmise, postulate, presume.
attribute:	feature, mark, quality, trait, peculiarity, characteristic, idiosyncracy, mannerism.
avoid:	escape, eschew, shun, evade, elude.
ban:	bar, debar, prevent, prohibit, stop, forbid, interdict.
barren:	futile, sterile, fruitless, profitless, vain, infertile, feckless, impotent, bleak, jejune, untenable, aborted, stillborn.
beat:	flog, lash, spank, whip, thrash, flagellate, scourge (archaic).
begin:	start, commence, initiate, launch inaugurate, institute.
benevolent:	kind, generous, genial, altruistic, helpful, compassionate,
bewilder:	puzzle, perplex, confuse, dumbfounded, surprise, mystify, amaze, stun, astound, shock, nonplus, flabbergast, confound, astonish, obfuscate.

brave:	courageous, dauntless, fearless, gallant, heroic, intrepid, bold, confident, daring, foolhardy, smug, poised, valiant, valorous, plucky, undaunted, audacious.
brief:	terse, coincide, precise, laconic, succinct, bridged, short, curtailed, exact, accurate.
cancel:	annul, rescind, repeal, discontinue, erase, delete, efface, eradicate, expunge, obliterate.
capture	arrest, catch, nab, trap, apprehend, round-up.
careful:	prudent, tactful, discreet, frugal, mindful, diligent, cautious, thrifty, recherché, meticulous, scrupulous, punctilious, wary.
casual:	haphazard, desultory, random, aimless, artless, disorderly, care-free.
charm:	attract, captivate, bewitch, enchant, draw, win, fascinate, entice, cajole, jolt.
chew:	grind, champ, chomp, gnash, masticate, crush.
clear:	conspicuous, apparent, obvious, ostensible, visible, seen, plain, noticeable, distinct, lucid, definite, explicit, transparent, patent, crystalline, pellucid.
cold:	frigid, gelid, icy, chilly, cool, chilled.
collect:	assemble, gather, convene, muster, mass, conglomerate, harmonize.
compulsory:	obligatory, imperative, mandatory, binding, deregueur.
consistent:	static, constant, unchanging, invariable, permanent, immutable, indifferent, continuous.
core:	kernel, heart, hub, middle, midst, crux, center, nub, nucleus, pith.
criticize:	excoriate, censure, judge, appreciate, castigate.
dangerous:	inimical, detrimental, jeopardizing, hazardous, risky, injurious, harmful.
deceit:	guile, cunningness, crafty, trick.

destroy:	demolish, exterminate, wreck, eradicate, annihilate, raze, uproot, ruin, extripate, kill, assassinate, execute, butcher, dispatch, massacre, slay, slaughter, murder, liquidate, damage.
egregious:	remarkable, outstanding, unique, prominent, august, distinguished, dominant, foremost, paramount, popular, predominant, exceptional, eminent, renowned, famous, respected, celebrated, noted, distinctive.
eminent:	illustrious, great, notable, distinct, noble, famous, noteworthy, distinguished, significant, august, majestic, reputable, pre-eminent, prominent, renowned.
encroach:	intrude, insinuate, invade, trespass, infringe, violate.
enormous:	gigantic, huge, immense, thumping, prodigious, magnificent, bit, mammoth, macro, giant, hefty, massive, vast, grand, ponderous, tremendous, stupendous, colossal, Herculean.
estrange:	exorcise, banish, ostracize, evict, anathematize, excommunicate, expel, eject, deport, expatriate, rusticate, exile, isolate, alienate, oust, remove, dismiss.
error:	flaw, evil, fault, indiscretion, misdeed, wrong, transgression, sin, defect, blemish.
examine:	assess, probe, catechize, evaluate, audit, inspect, investigate, scrutinize, review, x-ray, grill.
extract:	excerpt, quote, quotation, blurb.
extravagant:	wasteful, prodigal, luxurious, opulent, ostentations, affluent, wealthy, luxuriant, rich, thriftless, florid.
fertile:	productive, fecund, prolific, fruitful, viable, proliferous.
filthy:	sordid, fetid, rotten, squalid, putrid, stinking, dirty, horrid, rancid, stale.

finish:	complete, conclude, close, end, finalize, consummate, round-off.
foolish:	imbecile, stupid, weak-minded, asinine, idiotic, silly, moronic, dull, unintelligent, blunt.
forgive:	pardon, tolerate, overlook, excuse, condone, remit.
force:	compel, coerce, oblique, constrain, necessitate
foretell:	predict, prophecy, prognosticate, divine, forecast, augur.
frank:	ingenious, outspoken, candid, bluff, sincere, naive, blunt.
friend:	acquaintance, buddy, confidant, mate, comrade, crony, chum, companion, clique.
funny:	comic, witty, humorous, comical, jocose, waggish, jocular, facetious, droll.
fury:	indignation, wrath, anger, rage, ire.
grapple:	snatch, grasp, clutch, clasp, grip, seize.
grave:	tomb, cenotaph, mausoleum, sepulcher, vault.
greedy:	avaricious, envious, gluttonous, acquisitive, mangy, miserly, rapacious, parsimonious tight, sparing, niggardly, chary, avid.
happy:	delighted, glad, rapturous, joyous, gay, ecstatic, elated, euphoric, exhilarated, blithe, cheerful, excited, exuberant, jubilant.
harmful:	un-healthful, un-healthy, insalubrious, unwholesome, injurious, ruinous, unprofitable.
hinder:	mar, encumber, hamper, impede, obstruct, debar, prevent, intercept, stop, bar, barricade, block, interpose, interrupt.
hotel:	motel, saloon, inn, café, bar, restaurant, cafeteria, luncheonette, lounge, tavern (old use).
human:	humane, sympathetic, benign, charitable, philanthropic, hospitable, compassionate, humanitarian.
imitate:	mimic, copy, ape, impersonate.

impromptu:	unplanned, impulsive, improvished, spontaneous, extemporaneous, unpremeditated, sudden.
instill:	implant, imbue, infuse, inculcate, ingrain, inseminate, establish, fix, entrench.
instinctive:	spontaneous, innate, natural, intrinsic, intuitive, potential, inherent, congenital, hereditary, genetic.
intelligent:	bright, clever, brilliant, splendid, radiant, sparkling, excellent, refulgent, lambent, witty, astute, shrewd, adroit, dexterous.
laud:	extol, eulogize, praise, acclaim, applaud, endorse, approve.
laugh:	grin, guffaw, chuckle, smile, chortle, titter, snugger, giggle, snicker, simper, smirk.
law:	regulation, canon, ordinance, commandment, constitution, statute, code.
lead:	guide, conduct, pilot, steer, direct, navigate, engineer, pioneer.
link:	join, unite, attach, couple, bind, connect.
look:	watch, stare, view, gaze, glance, peer, glare, observe, inspect, see, examine.
mean:	imply, connote, denote, suggest, indicate, signify, symbolize, signal, entail, presuppose, conjecture.
meditate:	ponder, reason, speculate, cognate, excogitate, deliberate, ruminant, reflect, think.
mix:	amalgamate, combine, compose, join, liaise, confederate, conglomerate, alloy, compound, harmonize, blend.
move:	go, walk, run, trek, advance, sneak, slink, lurk, creep, skulk, scrawl, wobble, hop, jump, progress, proceed, approach.
noisy:	blatant, rough, boisterous, clamorous, rumbustious, rambunctious, obstreperous, loud, hilarious, vociferous.
novice:	apprentice, beginner, trio, neophyte, new-comer.

old:	primitive, outdated, obsolete, discontinuous, olden, archaic, anachronistic, crude, outlandish, outmoded, ancient, artless, uncivilized, unsophisticated, naïve, savage, barbarous.
opaque:	vague, obscure, hidden, concealed, dark, mysterious, abstruse, arcane, cryptic, recondite, nebulous, amorphous, unclear, cloudy.
peak:	apex, climax, acme, zenith, summit, top, pinnacle.
periodic:	occasional, incessant, continual, timely, intermittent, repeated, ephemeral, temporary, remittent, sporadic.
persist:	persevere, continue, endure, last, survive, weather, importune.
polite:	courteous, civil, decent, modest, decorous, refined, moderate, respectful, urbane, reverent, sophisticated, cultured, suave, genteel.
pollute:	adulterate, spoil, vitiate, contaminate, pervert, corrupt.
poor:	destitute, indigent, penniless, necessitous, needy, penurious.
potential:	latent, convert, implicit, unspoken, tacit.
proud:	arrogant, impevious, haughty, commanding, boastful.
quiet:	calm, unruffled, clement, docile, restful, amiable, gentle, placid, tranquil, serene, still, silent, peaceful, taciturn, subdued.
read:	scan, skim, peruse, study, browse, decipher, decode.
reasonable:	genuine, authentic, germane, real, actual, rational, sensible, valid, lucid, correct, relevant, sagacious, plausible, shrewd.
rebuke:	reprimand, admonish, censure, reproach, reprove, warn, caution.

salary:	wage, stipend, compensation, reward, emolument, pay, honorarium, perquisite, pittance, remuneration, commission, allowance.
scornful:	contemptuous, impudent, disdainful, insolent, supercilious, scurry.
search:	seek, hunt, track, comb, ransack, explore, scout.
secret:	hidden, concealed, implicit, inconspicuous, opaque, imperceptible, mysterious, unknown.
serious:	grave, earnest, sober, sedate, solemn, staid, committed, devoted.
skilful:	adroit, dexterous, graceful, clever, resourceful, ingenious, competent.
steal:	pilfer, rob, extort, prowl, milk, embezzle, dupe, cheat.
stagger:	shiver, quake, wobble, shake, tremble, waver, shudder, quiver, stammer.
stereotype:	prototype, replica, ideal, archetype, pattern, facsimile, model, type, photocopy.
strict:	stern, austere, astringent, grim, cruel, rigid, forbidding, severe, harsh, stringent.
stubborn:	obstinate, adamant, obdurate, heady, pertinacious, disobedient, recalcitrant, headstrong, stiff-necked, rebellious, impenitent.
temporal:	earthly, worldly, carnal, terrestrial, material, bodily, corporeal, mundane, physical, corporal,. Natural, fleshy, mesomorphic.
unbelievable:	incredible, incredulous, implausible, doubtful, blurred, suspicious, vague, unreliable, foggy, muddled.
uninterested:	lethargic, indifferent, listless, unenthusiastic, lackadaisical, languid, languorous.
unreasonable:	absurd, frivolous, ludicrous, insane, irrelevant, ridiculous, grotesque, bizarre, preposterous, foolish, senseless, farcical, irrational.

urgent:	immediate, quick, sudden, emergent, exigent, speedy.
victimize:	cheat, defraud, con, fleece, swindle
vindicate:	defend, rebut, validate, prove, justify.
weak:	feeble, faint, frail, fragile, flimsy, tenuous, deliberated, decrepit, infirm, vulnerable.
wicked:	vicious, cruel, ferocious, depraved, corrupt, merciless, vile, evil, nefarious, villainous, notorious, ruthless, unforgiving, infamous, heinous, vindictive, sullen, vengeful.
worry:	anxiety, angst, misgiving, disquieted, dread, apprehension, foreboding, uneasiness, fidget.
zealous:	eager, enthusiastic, avid, desirous, intent, keen, earnest, fervent, committed, devoted.

CAUTION: It should be noted with care that words that are synonyms share a common concept but their exact meanings vary either semantically, lexically, grammatically or contextually. Consider the following examples.

(i) brilliant, clever, right, intelligent.

In examples given above, brilliant can be used to refer to females, clever to males, while bright and intelligent may be used to refer to both males, females and non-living things. All these synonyms have a common concept – knowledgeable or witty. The difference is that they are not all used in the same way.

Example:
(a) He is a clever boy.
(b) She is a brilliant girl.
(c) Both Tom and Abigail are bright students.
(d) My uncle and his six children are very intelligent.
(e) Tomorrow may be a bright day.

(ii) beautiful, handsome, nice

In this second example, beautiful, is normally used to refer to females or objects but handsome usually refers to males. Nice can be used for both as in: She is beautiful. He is a handsome boy. Both the girl and her father are nice-looking.

(iii) Condiment, ingredient, paraphernalia, regalia.

Each of these synonyms generally refers to the component parts of a single concept. Condiment refers to items used in preparing food, e.g. pepper, salt, onions, fish, and so on; ingredient implies the component parts of mixture e.g. the ingredients of soap-making;

Paraphernalia means items or small possessions used for one's hobby or technical work, e.g. spanner, hammer, wood, chisel and regalia denotes emblems of royalty, e.g. scepter, crown, orb, robe, and so on.

From the examples given above, it is clear that although synonyms have close reference points in terms of the general meaning, their usages differ slightly or greatly. Users should, therefore, avoid using synonyms in anticipation of their meaning without adequate knowledge of both the connotative and denotative meanings of the words. This is because all words differ in usage and rarely do two words mean exactly the same thing. Although there may exist few cases where two or more words mean exactly the same thing, such words are continually bending their meanings towards new usages. So the possibility of retaining the original meaning of a word is relatively difficult. Thus, the knowledge of synonyms is very necessary so as to avoid ambiguity, tautology or other related errors in grammar.

ANTONYMS

As defined earlier, antonyms are words that are opposite in meaning to another in the same language. There are numerous antonyms in English Language and, like synonyms, they originated from other languages that streamed into English during its formative years. English antonyms are almost inexhaustible, so only a few antonyms will be treated in this section.

Word	Antonyms
absorb:	eject, emit, reject, disgorge, disperse, excrete, dissipate, exude, repulse, resent.
add:	subtract, reduce, lesson, deduct, abstract.
adequate:	inadequate, insufficient, mean, deficient, meager, miniature, minimal.
admire:	despise, disdain, abhor, loathe, scorn, detest
affirm:	dispute, doubt, contradict, demur, refute, rebut
afraid:	bold, aggressive, pushful, forward, audacious, brave, calm, confident, foolhardy
agree:	disagree, dissent, cavil, bicker, object, quibble
ancient:	modern, contemporary, current, recent.
arrest:	free, emancipate, release, liberate.
bold:	fearful, afraid, alarmed, apprehensive, frightened, scared, aghast, terror-stricken, anxious, timid, cowardly, daunted.
comfort:	bother, disturb, pester, harass, plague, worry, trouble, fret.
confront:	escape, flee, abscond, retreat.
doubtful:	credible, plausible, certain, clear, sure, definite, believable.
existent:	dead, defunct, extinct, deceased, departed, lifeless.
flexible:	rigid, fixed, unchanged, set, inflexible, dogmatic.
forget:	remember, recall, memorize, recollect, remind, retain, reproduce, cram.
genuine:	artificial, synthetic, false, untrue, faked, unauthentic, counterfeit, unreal.
hostile:	cordial, friendly, gregarious, amiable, affable, sociable, hospitable, humane.
humane:	brutal, cruel, bestial, sadistic, nasty, barbarous, wicked, inhuman, barbaric.

idiot:	genius, intellectual, sage, savant.
ignorant:	aware, conscious, mindful, cognizant.
indolent:	diligent, hardworking, skilful, assiduous, industrious, sedulous.
large:	minute, microscopic, infinitesimal, miniature, minuscule, micro.
maintain:	relinquish, cede, abdicate, abandon, renounce, resign, surrender, yield, desert.
mature:	immature, inexperienced, childish, infantile, juvenile, puerile, trivial, youthful.
meticulous:	negligent, remiss, careless, heedless, sloppy.
mortal:	immortal, deathless, imperishable, timeless, undying, ageless, eternal
obscure:	renowned, famous, celebrated, noted, clear, obvious, notorious, apparent, ostensible, seen.
persuade:	dissuade, discourage, deter, divert
protection:	danger, jeopardy, menace, hazard, risk, peril, threat
publish:	hide, conceal, secrete, censor, with-hold
repair:	harm, damage, disable, hurt, injure, destroy, incapacitate, exacerbate.
scarce:	sufficient, abundant, adequate, enough, surplus, ample, copious, available
sensitive:	callous, indifferent, lethargic, uninterested, lackadaisical
selfish:	generous, lavish, liberal, bountiful, magnanimous
significant:	marginal, minor, negligible, inconsequential, nugatory, peripheral, piddling, trifling, insignificant, infinitesimal.
tolerant:	rigid, severe, austere, stain, vindictive, sullen, vengeful, unforgiving, strict.

Beside the list of antonyms enumerated above, there are other English antonyms that could be considered in pairs. This is not, however, a rule. It is designed to guide the reader to develop his/her vocabulary and to aid memory. Here are few of such antonyms:

Word	Antonyms
accept	reject
acquit	convict
broad	narrow
build	destroy
convince	dissuade
denounce	advocate
displease	gratify
display	conceal
essential	unnecessary
explicit	vague
feeble	strong
flagrant	fetid
foreign	domestic
fraudulent	upright
generous	mean
hide	exhibit
indolent	hardworking
nervous	relaxed
novice	expert
opulent	poor
rigid	flexible
unruffled	worry
valuable	valueless
vice	virtue

CHAPTER THIRTEEN
CONCORD

Concord is the agreement which exists between different grammatical elements relating to number, person, gender, tense, and voice. It is a synthetic feature of language the purpose of which is to bring about harmony between the subject and the verb, the pronoun and its antecedent as well as help maintain consistency in sentence construction as regards person, number, gender, tense, mood and voice.

The major rules of concord that will be considered for discussion in this section are:
(a) Concord of number between subject and verb;
(b) Pronoun/antecedent concord;
(c) Shifts in construction vis-a-vis person, number, gender, tense, and voice.

Concord of Number Between Subject and Verb
This is an important rule of concord in English. The major rules governing this kind of concord are as outlined below.
(i) Singular subject requires singular verb.
Example:
The lawyer talks about the case with conviction.

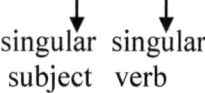
singular singular
 subject   verb

The worker has agreed to conceal the secret.

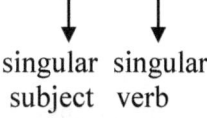
singular singular
 subject   verb

(ii) Plural subject requires plural verb: Example:

Lawyers talk about the case with conviction.
plural plural
subject verb

The workers have agreed to conceal the secret.
    plural plural
    subject verb

In the examples cited above, it is clear that a noun ending in -s denotes plural while verb ending in –s indicates the third person singular. Relatively, the auxiliary verb "has" is singular whereas "have" is plural.

E.g.   Singular subjects and singular verbs:

(i)   The goat eats grass.

    singular singular
    subject verb

(ii)   He rings the bell.

    singular singular
    subject verb

(iii)   Goats eat grass

    plural plural
    subject verb

(iv)   They ring the bell

    plural plural
    subject verb

The subject/verb concord occurs in various ways as discussed below.

(i)   Separate subjects joined by "and" usually require plural verb.
Example:
Ben and Philip **are** serious students.
However, there is another side to this rule. When both subjects refer to the same person or when one of the subjects is in apposition (i.e. if the second subject adds meaning to the first), the verb in that sentence is singular.
Example:
His teacher and sponsor **is** in support of his action.
Professor Donald and Vice-Chancellor **has** approved Ike's application for study leave.

Note: If the two subjects in these sentences are preceded by modifiers respectively, then the verbs must be plural.
Example:
His teacher and his sponsor **are** in support of his action.
Professor Donald and the Vice-Chancellor **have** approved his application for study leave.

(ii)   Singular subjects joined by or, nor, but, either or and neither nor take singular verbs.
Example:
Mr. Simeon or his wife **is** expected at the board meeting.
It is not his wife but his mother that **thinks** he is irresponsible.
Either his brother or his son **is** going to succeed in the examination.

Note: If one of the subjects is singular and the other plural, or when both subjects differ in person, the verb agrees with the subject nearer to it.
Example:
Either Henry or you **are** to go.
Here, "you" (the nearer subject to the verb) is plural and so the following verb takes plural form.
On the other hand, the sentence reads thus:

Either you or Henry **is** to go.
In this case, the nearer subject "Henry" is singular and so takes the singular verb "**is**".
(iii) When compound subjects joined by "and" function as a single unit, the following verb takes singular form:
Example:
Rice and beans **makes** a palatable meal.
Bread and butter **is** best taken as breakfast.
Sixes and sevens **is** merely an idiomatic expression
Success and failure **is** bound to occur in one's life.
Trial and error **is** necessary for a successful career.
(iv) A singular subject followed immediately by words or phrases of addition such as: in addition to, with, together with, and as well as requires singular verb.
Example:
The woman with children **has** promised to visit us.
His last statement, in addition to a previous one, **is** false.
The director together with his wife **was** praised.
The secretary as well as the president **is** accused.
(v) A singular subject followed by a plural modifier such as "these" and "those" still takes singular verb.
Example:
The attitude of these men **is** apparently hostile.
The leader of those rebel forces **has** been captured.
Note: The expressions "of these men" and "of those rebel forces" are just modifying phrases which do not obstruct the relationship between the subject and the verb of the sentences.
If the expression involves the partitive genitive construction (i.e. the grammatical construction that expresses part of a whole concept), then, the verb has to take the singular form.
Example:
One of my biros **is** not writing well.
In one of these bags **was** a loaf of bread.
One of the students **speaks** frankly.

One of the thieves **has** been arrested.

Note that in the examples given here, the pronoun "one" is the part that is affected by the verb and not the nouns in the prepositional phrase.

(vi) Indefinite pronouns such as anyone, anybody, each, either, every, everyone, everybody, no-one, nobody, none, nothing and everything generally require singular verbs.

Example:
Anyone who *does* that **is** foolish.
Each of them **is** bound to pay the price
Nobody **admits** seeing the thief

Moreover, expressions such as all, any, none, most and some may take either singular or plural verbs depending on the sense implied.

Example:
Any of the suggestions **is** satisfactory.
Any of the workers **are** qualified to apply.
Some of his books **are** classic.
All **is** well that ends well.
All of them **are** free to take the test.

(vii) Collective nouns such as family, jury, people, team, choir, police, class, group, crowd, committee, army, congregation, council and audience take singular verb when they function as single units and plural verb when the members function independently as noun of multitude.

Example:
The family **holds** her annual meeting today.
The police **are** holding their plenary session.
The factory staff **are** really very hard-working.
Samson **is** a renowned staff of the company.
The jury **believes** in unalloyed justice.

The same rule in (vii) above applies to nominal phrases such as "a great deal of", "the rest of", "a part of", "a number of", and so on.

Example:

A number of items **have** been received.
The number of items in the store **is** negligible.
The rest of the story **is** untrue.
The rest of the books **are** very useful.

Nominal expressions involving collective units and indicating plural nouns mainly take singular verbs. Such expressions include "a collection of", "a body of", a team of", a "piece of", "a handful of".

Example:
A team of inspectors **has** been dispatched.
A collection of books **has** been ordered.
A piece of information **has** been received.
A body of knowledge on this issue **seems** necessary.
A band of soldiers **arrives** Lagos today.

(viii) Nouns which appear to be plural in form but singular in meaning take singular verbs. Such nouns include: Mathematics, Physics, Politics, Electronics, Chasis, Economics, the United Nations, alms, series, droughts, emphasis, arrears, statistics, science, ethics, scissors, trousers, aesthetics, athletics measles, news, beans, and so on.

Example:
Mathematics **is** my favorite subject.
No news **is** good news.
The statistics of those items **has** been taken.
The United Nations **has** send an envoy to the city.

(ix) Measurements of weights and distance as well as periods of time and amount of money are generally regarded as single units and, therefore, require singular verbs.

Example:
Twenty kilograms of rice **is** not enough for the visitors.
One thousand miles **is** a long distance to travel.
Four million Naira **appears** too meagre to complete a major project.

(x)   Compound expressions that are plural in form but singular in meaning take singular verb.
   Example:
   A five-member committee *has* been appointed.
   A thirty-year-old police officer **has** been killed.
   A four-year development plan **seems** a better option.
Note: In the sentences above, the compound expressions only serve as modifying phrases to the head-nouns.
(xi)   The title of a single work such as a newspaper, a magazine, a book or a film which appears to be plural in form still takes singular verb.
   Example:
   Daily Times **attracts** a wider audience.
   The Great Ponds **is** an interesting African novel.
   "Galatians" is one of the books in the Bible.
(xi)   Sometimes, the position of the subject is intriguing particularly when the subject follows the verb in sentences involving expressions such as "there is", "there are" or "were". Special care should be taken, therefore, to determine the subject and to make sure they agree with verb.
   Example:
   On the King's retinue **were** several dignitaries.
   In one of the vessels **was** an item of furniture.
   There **are** in the class a lecturer and a student.
   There **is** in the boardroom an enlarged photograph.
   (xii)   When the complement of the verb "to be" affects the number of the verb, then the verb takes either the singular or plural form depending on its position. The verb "to be" include: is, are, was, were, been, being, am, be.
   Example:
   Books **are** her chief source of enjoyment.
   Her chief source of enjoyment **is** books.

(xiv) A phrase modifying the subject does not influence the form of the verb.
Example:
This box with four tyres **is** mine.
The table with broken legs **belongs** to him.

(xv) Irregular plurals occurring in Latin or Greek words take plural verb.
Example:
The bourgeoisie **are** more popular in politics.
The stadia **are** colourfully decorated.

(xvi) Pronominal expressions involving the form of the verb "to be" (e.g. I am, he is, you are, they were, and so on.) which are separated by an appositive phrase or the relative clause always collocate, and thereby, agree with their accompanying element.
Example:
It is **you**, the guardian and sponsor, that **are** at fault.
You, who know the technique, **are** to educate the others.
I, the author and publisher, **am** to sign for the contract.
They, the members of the council, **were** to rebut the allegation.
He, the Accountant-General, **is** responsible for the fraud.

Note: The pronominal expressions given above still retain their normal positions in the absence of an interrupter or an appositive. But in questions, their positions are in the reverse, e.g.

Who **am I**?
How **are they**?
What **are you** doing?
"Whom do men say that **I** the Son of Man **Am**?
(Matthew, 16,p.13).

Pronoun/Antecedent Concord

A pronoun must agree with its antecedent in gender, number and case. (An antecedent is a noun or a phrase to which following pronoun refers).
Example:
Glory was so sick that she could not take her tests.

    antecedent   pronoun

The president has said that he will perform the ceremony.

    antecedent   pronoun

All the students acknowledged that they were guilty.

    antecedent   pronoun

Pronominal expressions should agree in person with their antecedents.
Example:
Everyone is expected to do his job.

    singular   singular

All of them came with their books.

    plural   plural

There are various general rules governing this kind of agreement. Here are some of them.

(i)   Singular pronouns are used to refer to such antecedents as man, woman, cousin, person, kind, sort, each, either, neither, another, anybody, somebody, someone, one, every, everyone, everybody, none, nobody, no-one, nothing, anything, everything, and something.
Example:

If a man realizes his fault, he has to plead for pardon.

singular   singular
antecedent   pronoun

My cousin affirmed that those books were his.

singular   singular
antecedent   pronoun

Everyone of them agreed that he was at fault.

singular   singular
antecedent   pronoun

(i) The plural pronoun is used to refer to two or more antecedents joined by "and".

Example:
Henry and James acknowledged that those items were theirs.

plural antecedent   plural pronoun

The students agreed to hand in their notes.

plural   plural
antecedent   pronoun

(ii). Two or more singular antecedents joined by "either or" or "neither nor" require singular pronoun.

Example:
Neither Henry nor James has greed that the mistake is his.

singular   singular
antecedent   pronoun

Either Henry or James has forgotten his books.

singular   singular

        antecedent   pronoun

Note: If any of the antecedents joined by "nor" or "or" is singular and the other plural, the pronoun agrees with the nearer antecedent.

Example:
Neither the students nor the teacher agrees that the books are his.

                        singular   nearer
                        pronoun   antecedent

Neither the teacher nor the students agree that the books are theirs.

                        nearer   plural
                        antecedent   pronoun

(iii) Collective nouns are referred to by singular or plural pronouns depending on the sense in which they are used.

Example:
The staff are electing their leader.

   plural   plural
   antecedent   pronoun

In this case, staff is seen as constituting individual members.

The team is electing her leader.

   singular   singular
   antecedent   pronoun

Here, team is viewed as a collective unit.

The police is conducting her investigation.

   singular   singular
   antecedent   pronoun

The police have agreed to do their work

   plural   plural
   antecedent   pronoun

(iv) Agreement involving relative pronouns such as who, which and that requires tact to make appropriate construction. The relative pronoun "who" is used when the antecedent is a person; "which" is used when the antecedent is a thing or an animal; and "that" is used to refer to a person, an animal or a thing.
   Example:
   The man spoke to the **girl who** found the items.
   The **radio which** was stolen had been found.
   The **story that** I told you is anonymous.
   The **teacher who** was sacked has been recalled.
   In the examples given above, "who" refers to girl, "which" refers to radio, "that" refers to story and "that" refers to teacher respectively.
(v) A noun or pronoun used predicatively agrees in case with the words to which it refers.
   Example:
   They elected **him president.**
   In this sentence, the predicate nominative "president" functions in the accusative case and agrees with the objective pronoun "him".

Virtually, on a more specific note, a pronoun must agree with its antecedent in number, gender and case. The basic rules governing this aspect of concord include the following.

(a) Number: If a person replaces a noun, the number indicating the noun replaced must be represented by the pronoun that replaces it.
   Example:
   The president has agreed to speed up his job.
          ↓   ↓
       singular   singular
   All the men have promised to contribute their quota.
              ↓   ↓
           plural   plural

Many politicians are ready to support their candidates.
    ↓   ↓
   plural   plural

The manager promised to pay everyone his due.
           ↓ ↓
         singular singular

Two of the boys came back and they accepted the offer
↓   ↓
plural   plural

Hundreds of Naira was spent but it was not enough for the job.
     ↓   ↓
   singular   singular

Gender:
 If the noun which the pronoun replaces indicates masculine, feminine or neuter gender, the pronoun replacing it must also mark these genders accordingly.

Example:
The book is very comprehensive. It contains all the facts I need
  ↓   ↓
 singular   singular
 neuter   neuter

I believe you must have seen Emily. I hope to see her, too.
          ↓   ↓
        singular   singular
        feminine   feminine

We spoke to the boy. The management has promised to help him.
      ↓   ↓
    singular   singular
    masculine   masculine

Basic English Grammar and Usage

The dogs barked continually. They were provoked by the cat
↓ ↓
plural   plural
neuter   neuter

The girls accused the man of bigotry. They detest his attitude.
↓ ↓
plural   plural
feminine feminine

When our brothers speak, we normally admire them.
↓ ↓
plural   plural
masculine masculine

(c) **Case:** A subject noun should be replaced by subject pronoun and an object noun by an object pronoun.

Example:

The boy has agreed to come. He has already given his consent.
↓ ↓
subject   subject

I met Bisi and Anayo, but they refused to come with me.
↓ ↓
subject   subject

The company sent some books to Amina, but we did not see her.
↓ ↓
object   object

The court directed us to see our clients and tell them to pay fines.
↓ ↓
plural   plural
object   object

248

Shifts in Construction

This third rule of concord emphasizes the consistent use of grammatical elements involving gender, number, person, tense, and voice (cf Oluikpe,1981). Any unnecessary shift in construction from one element to another may affect meaning or sometimes render the structure of the whole sentence less meaningful. Let us now examine each of these elements closely.

Gender

There are principally three genders in English namely masculine, feminine and neuter. Masculine gender makes reference to males, feminine gender refers to females; and the neuter gender is used to denote things, places or animals. Note that the feminine gender is also used to indicate collective nouns such as army, jury, team, government, and so on. Sentence constructions which involve unnecessary shift from one gender to another should be avoided.

Consider the following examples

(a) If Victor wants to win the case, let her go to court.
        ↓   ↓
     Masculine   Feminine

(b) The goat died before she was buried.
        ↓   ↓
     Neuter   feminine

(c) Nigeria has its citizens to protect.
        ↓   ↓
     feminine neuter

The shifts in construction from one gender to another in the sentences cited above make them incorrect. The sentences can be corrected as follows:

(a) If Victor wants to win the case, let him go to court
        ↓   ↓
     masculine   masculine

(b)   The goat died before it was buried.
            ↓   ↓
          neuter   neuter

(c)   Nigeria has her citizens to protect.
            ↓   ↓
         feminine feminine

Number:
   The English number system is indicated by two terms namely, singular and plural. Singular marks one and plural denotes more than one. The rule of concord requires that there should be consistency in indicating number in a single sentence. Examine the following sentences.

(a)   The children are crying for his books
            ↓   ↓
          plural   singular

(b). The three units have its days of meeting.
                   ↓   ↓
                plural   singular

(c)   The student is meeting with their lecturers.
            ↓   ↓
         singular   plural

Grammatically, these sentences are incorrect. The correct forms will be as follows:

(a)   The children are crying for their books.
            ↓   ↓
          plural   plural

(b)   The three units have their days of meeting.
            ↓   ↓
          plural   plural

(c)   The student is meeting with his lecturers.
            ↓   ↓
         singular   singular

250

Person:
Pronouns are marked by three persons namely 1st person, 2nd person and third person. Generally, person is linked with number thus there are 1st person singular and plural, 2nd person singular and plural, and third person singular and plural forms respectively. These include:

1st person pronouns: namely; I, me (as singular), and we, us, our (as plural);

2nd person pronouns e.g. you (singular) and you (plural);

3rd person pronoun such as he, she, it (as singular) and they, them, and so on, (as plural).

The rule of concord states that there should be consistent use of either 1st person, 2nd person or 3rd person pronouns without unnecessary shift from one person to another in a single construction.

Consider the following sentences:
(a)   If one fails his examinations, you are constrained to weep.

      3rd person   2nd person

(b)   I detest sleeping late because it makes you weak.

1st person   2nd person
singular   singular

(c)   He prefers art subjects to science because it helps me read law.

3rd person   1st person
singular   singular

The sentences cited above are not grammatically correct because of the shift from one person to another. They can be corrected as follows:

Basic English Grammar and Usage

(a) If one fails his examinations, one is constrained to weep.

       ↓   ↓

3rd person   3rd person
singular   singular

(b) I detest sleeping late because it makes me weak

    ↓   ↓

1st person   1st person

(c) He prefers art subjects to science because it helps him read law.

  ↓   ↓

3rd person   3rd person
singular   singular

Tense:

      Tense is a verb form that establishes the relationship between the time of an action, event or state of affairs and the moment of speaking about the event or state of affairs. There are principally three tenses in English namely past tense, present tense and "future" tense. Unnecessary shift from one tense to the other in a single sentence (except where the inclusion of such tenses are deemed useful or needful) should be avoided.

Consider the following examples:

(a) I came to the school in the morning but I am too tired to write.

     ↓   ↓

past tense   present tense

(b) She is speaking to you but you were not listening.

        ↓   ↓

    present tense   past tense

(c) We saw the policeman who shoots the thief.

      ↓   ↓

    past tense   present tense

These sentences are wrong and can be corrected in the following ways:

(a) I came to the school in the morning but I was too tired to write.

    past tense   past tense

(b)   She is speaking to you but you are not listening.

            present tense   present tense

(c)   We saw the policeman who shot the thief

            past tense   present tense

However, there are exceptions to this rule. For instance, in most cases, when the verb is preceded by "to", the tense usually takes the present form.

Example:

I had hoped to see Mr. Clinton to discuss the issue.

Again when the expression "high time" or "about time" is used, the following verb usually takes the past form (except it is preceded by "to"), as in:

It is high time we feared God.

                    OR

It is high time to fear God.

It is about time we stopped working in the company.

Note that all the three tenses (the past, the present and the future) could be employed in a single sentence but the user should be able to handle the them properly so as to avoid irrelevant or unnecessary shift in tenses.

Examine the following sentence:

The author tells us that he knew the problems he was likely to encounter if he should disobey the publisher.

In the sentence above, "tells" is in the present tense, "knew" is in the past, "was" is past tense and "should disobey" marks futurity. Yet, the sentence is correct because of the way it is handled.

Voice

Voice is the grammatical category used to denote whether the verb portrays the subject as performing the action on the one hand, or the subject is the recipient of the action of the verb on the other. When the subject of the sentence is presented as the one performing the action, the verb is said to be in the *active voice*. But if the subject is merely receiving the action of the verb, then the verb in that case is said to be in the *passive voice*.

Example:

The Police Inspector *cautioned* the Sergeant.

active voice

The Sergeant was *cautioned* by the Police Inspector.

passive voice

It is however, apparent that any careless or unnecessary shift from one voice to another may render the sentence "weak" or less meaningful. Consider the following examples:

(a) She *thought* quickly, *raised up* her hand, and the answer *was given.*

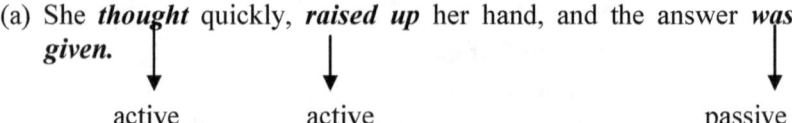

    active   active   passive

(b) He was *helped* by the children and he *thanked* them heartily.

        passive   active

(c)   The Police *hated* them but we *were encouraged*.

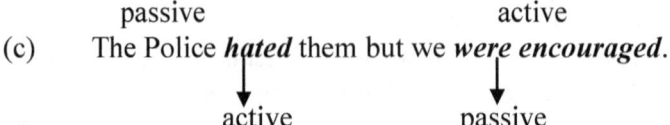

            active   passive

These sentences can be corrected s follows:
(a) She ***thought*** quickly, ***raised up*** her hand, and ***gave*** the answer.
        ↓   ↓   ↓
   active   active   passive

(b) The children ***helped*** immensely and he ***thanked*** them heartily.
               ↓   ↓
     active   active

Police ***hated*** them, but they ***encouraged*** us.
      ↓   ↓
  active   active

It should be noted too, that the use of active voice makes more meaningful and effective sentences than the passive voice. Therefore, it is advisable for writers to use more active voice in written discourses than the passive voice.

However, there could be a sentences which combine both the active and the passive voice effectively.

Example:
I stopped ***to greet*** him but was ***told*** by a neighbour that he ***has packed*** away.
         ↓   ↓   ↓
   active   passive   active

The manager ***spoke*** well and was ***supported*** by his colleagues.
              ↓   ↓
    active   passive

A GLOSSARY OF LINGUISTIC AND GRAMMATICAL TERMS

In this section, our intention is to provide a variety of linguistic and grammatical terms many of which we have used in the course of this work. The essence is to provide an avenue for quick reference if the reader encounters any problem in understanding any of the terminologies used within the text. Although those terms have been explained within the text, this glossary will provide a very quick reference point and make the task of understanding easy. Again, we consider that since references to these terms have been made in-text, there is no need to make them here again in order not to complicate the readers problems while reading through the definitions. For ease of reference, the items are arranged in alphabetical order.

Abstract: An abstract is a summary form of a short account of the principal points of a piece of writing, a lecture, a book, speech or a discourse.

Accentuation: Accentuation is the prominence (by means of stress) given to a syllable particularly in words of more than one syllable.

Accusative Case: This is the case of a noun or pronoun that serves as the object of the sentence or clause.

Active Voice: A verb is said to be in the active voice when it represents the subject as performing the action expressed in the sentence.

Adjective: An adjective is a word used to modify a noun or pronoun. It usually names quality and thereby defines or limits the meaning for the noun or pronoun. When adjectives occur before the word it qualifies, it is called attribute adjective but if it occurs within the predicate, it is called predicative adjective.

Adjectival Clause: An adjectival clause is a subordinate (dependent) clause that functions as an adjective and it depends on the main clause for its complete meaning. It is also referred to as relative clause. It is marked by such words like *that, which, who, whose* and so on.

Adjectival Phrase: This is a prepositional phrase that functions as an adjective. It can also be a group of adjectives strung together to qualify a head-noun.

Adjunct: An adjunct is an adverbial element, or an adverb added to qualify or define more vividly another word, phrase or clause in a sentence.

Adverb: An adverb is a lexical word that modifies verb, an adjective or another adverb even an entire clause.

Adverbial Clause: An adverbial clause is a dependent clause that functions as an adverb.

Adverbial Phrase: This is a prepositional phrase that functions as an adverb. It can also be a group of adverbs strung together to qualify an accompanying element (i.e. verb, adjective or another adverb).

Affix: An affix is a morpheme appearing either before, within or after the base of a word. It occurs before the base, it is called prefix, but if it appears after the base, it is known as suffix. If the affix is entrenched in-between the root of the word, it is either known as an infix or an interfix depending on its position within the word.

Antecedent: An antecedent is a word or an expression (more specially a noun, phrase or clause --- or sometimes a sentence) to which a following pronoun or adverb refers. Specially, in concord, it is the noun to which pronoun refers.

Appositive: An appositive is a word or group of words which identify, explain or make reference to another word or group of words earlier stated in an expression or sentence.

Appositive Phrase: This is a phrase which means the same thing as a noun or pronoun that preceded it. In essence, it is a noun phrase which modifies, explains or identifies the preceding noun or pronoun. E.g. Jackson, the footballer, has received a price. (Here "the footballer" is an appositive phrase because it means the same thing as Jackson.)

Article: The article functions as adjectives modifying the noun. There are two forms: the definite article, "the" is used to imply particular or definite context while the indefinite article, "a" or "an" marks generalization and imply indefinition. Note that the indefinite article "a" is used before a noun starting with a consonant

	sound while "an" is used before a noun begun with a vowel sound.
Aspect:	An aspect refers to variation in the form of verbs or verb phrases. It is used to show whether an action is beginning, continuing through time, completed already or habitual in nature. There are principally four types namely inceptive, progressive, perfective and iterative aspects.
Auxiliary verb:	An auxiliary (otherwise called helping or supporting verb) helps the principal verb to form verb phrases. Examples include can, could, may, must, might, will, would, shall, should, dare, be, ought to, have, do, and so on. The forms of the verb "to be" include, is, am, are, was, were, been, being. These, too, function as auxiliary verbs. Sometimes they are referred to as modal auxiliary verbs.
Base:	A base is a morphemic element or the root of a word none of whose allomorphs contain open junctures such as affixes.
Clause:	A clause is a group of related words having a subject and a predicate verb and is distinctly complete and meaningful. The predicate usually contains a finite verb but the whole expression may function as a single part of speech. There are principally two types: the dependent or subordinate clause which depends on the main clause for its meaning, and the independent or co-ordinate clause which is independently

complete and serves as the main clause in the sentence. Three kinds can be identified in an English sentences namely adverbial clause, relative clause and noun clause.

Collective noun: A collective noun is the name of a group, class or collection of members the function as a single unit. Examples include jury, committee, congregation, team, council, and so on.

Comma splice: Comma splice implies the use of a comma instead of a full stop or semi-colon between main clauses not linked by a co-ordinating conjunction. In other words, the comma is used as the sole connection between two or more independent clauses instead of the period or the semi-colon.

Common noun: A common noun is the general name of any one of class of persons, animals, places or things. Examples: bed, table, man book, and so on.

Comparative Degree: The comparative degree is the antecedent of the positive degree but the precedent of the superlatve degree of adverbs or adjectives. It is used when comprison is made between two persons, plces or things.

Comparison: Comparison refers to the change in the form of an adjective or an adverb to denote difference in degree. There are three degrees of comparison namely: positive, comprative, and superlative.

Complement: A complement is the grammatical name given to words, phrases or clauses which

	follow linking verbs and completes the meaning to the verb begun by the subject. It is usually a noun, a pronoun or an adjective.
Complete Predicate:	The complete predicate is the predicate verb or verb phrase with its complements and modifiers.
Complete Subject:	The complete subject is the combination of the simple subject with all its modifiers.
Demonstrative Adjective:	A demonstrative adjective specifically points out the noun or pronoun it qualifies. They include these, this, that, those, such, some.
Demonstrative Pronoun:	A demonstrative pronoun points out a specific person, animal, place or thing. They are the same as demonstrative adjectives above but they function as pronouns.
Dependent Clause:	The dependent clause (otherwise called subordinate clause) is a group of words that has subject and finite verb. Although the subordinate clause does not occur independently, yet, it expresses a complete thought, has its subject and predicate, and functions as a single part of speech.
Direct Object:	The direct object in a sentence receives the immediate or direct action of the verb.
Exclamatory Sentence:	An exclamatory sentence is the one used to express strong feelings or sudden emotions such as joy, sorrow, excitement, pain or surprise. It usually ends with the exclamatory mark (!).
Expletive:	An expletive is an introductory word which fills in the place of the grammatical

	subject. The real subject appears after the verb. An expletive has no grammatical connection with any part of the sentence. The words "it" and "there" are commonly used as expletives.
Function Word:	This is a word with little or no lexical meaning which is used in combining other words into syntactic structure. Mostly, prepositions; conjunctions and interjections serve as function words.
Future Perfect Tense:	The future perfect tense denotes action that will be completed at some definite time in the future.
Future Tense:	The future tense is used to mark future time.
Gerund:	A gerund is a verbal (verb form) that functions as a noun. It usually takes the "-ing" form of the verb and is sometimes known as verb-noun.
Grammar:	Grammar is a branch of linguistic which deals with the organization of morphemic units into rule-governed and meaningful combinations larger than word. It involves rules which govern the combination of words, phrases or clauses into sentences. Grammar basically embody morphology and syntax.
Imperative Mood:	The imperative mood is the mood which expresses a command or a request.
Imperative Sentence:	An imperative sentence is one that gives command or makes a request. It usually ends with period or an exclamation mark.

Basic English Grammar and Usage

Indefinite Pronoun: An indefinite pronoun does not point out a definite person, place or thing. Examples include any, anyone, anybody, some, someone, somebody, no, no-one, nobody, every, everyone, everybody, most, all, many, and so on.

Independent Clause: An independent clause (main or co-ordinate clause) is a group of related words that have a subject and a predicate verb, and expresses a complete though. An independent clause is the equivalent of a simple sentence since it contains the subject and a finite verb.

Indicative Mood: The indicative mood of the verb is the one that is used to make a statement, to state a fact or to ask question.

Indirect Object: An indirect objects tells to whom or for what something is done. It normally occurs after the direct object or in the predicate part of the sentence.

Infinitive: An infinitive is a verbal (verb form) that is used as a noun, an adjective, or an adverb. It is normally preceded by the word "to" which is commonly called the marker (sign) of the infinitive.

Infinitive Phrase: An infinitive phrase is an infinitive with any complement or modifier that it may take, e.g. "to read"

Inflection: An inflection is a morphological element or a word form comprising a stem (root) and an inflectional suffix. In nouns, inflection is used to mark declensions as in plurals and possessives;, in verbs, it is used to denote conjugations as in tense,

	aspect, participle, gerund, contraction and singular forms, and in pronouns, it is used to signify mutations as in person, number and gender.
Interjection:	An interjection is a word or a phrase that expresses strong feeling or sudden emotion to show joy, sorrow, pain or surprise.
Interrogative adverb:	An interrogative adverb introduces a question and modifies a verb. Markers include words like where, when, why, and so on.
Interrogative pronoun:	This is a pronoun that is used to ask question. Markers include words like what, when, which, who, whose, who, and so on.
Interrogative Sentence:	This is the type of sentence that asks a question. Usually, an interrogative sentence ends with the question mark (?)
Intransitive verb:	An intransitive verb is a verb that does not take an object e.g. He <u>swims.</u> He <u>cries</u> bitterly.
Linking verb:	A linking verb (*otherwise called copulative verb) is one that is used to connect the subject with a word that explains or describes the subject (i.e. the complement). The explanatory word, which may be a noun, a pronoun or an adjective, usually follows the verb. Words like be, become, seem, sound, remain, look, and so on. are linking verbs.
Loose Sentence:	A loose sentence is a sentence which begins with the main fact and ends with the secondary idea. It does not keep the

	reader in suspense concerning the principal idea it expresses.
Misplaced Modifier:	A misplaced modifier is one that is incorrectly placed in a sentence. In that case, it attempts to modify the wrong word because it is placed nearer to it than to the correct word. It is also called dangling modifier.
Modifier:	A modifier is a word or group of words that limits or qualifies the meaning of another word. It my be a single word, a phrase or clause. It can also serve as an adjective or an adverb.
Mood:	Mood is the form that the verb takes to show the manner in which the action or state of being is to be regarded. There are three kinds namely indicative, imperative and subjunctive moods.
Morpheme:	A morpheme is the smallest morphological unit of a word or the minimal grammatical unit of a language.
Morphology:	Morphology is a branch of linguistics which deals with the study of morphemes of a language and how they are combined to form words.
Nominative Case:	The nominative case is the case of a noun or pronoun which serves s the subject of the sentence. Relatively, a predicate noun is also in the nominative case. However, nouns have no special form to denote the nominative case.
Non-restrictive Relative Clause:	A non-restrictive relative clause is a subordinate clause that is not essentially

	significant to the meaning of the sentence. The non-restrictive relative clause is normally marked off from the rest of the sentence by commas.
Noun:	A noun is the name of an animal, a person, a place or a thing (concept, action, idea, quality or object). As a lexical word, a noun is inflected in three ways, namely: to show the plural form; to indicate the possessive it, they) marks the person or thing spoken of.
Personal Pronoun:	A personal pronoun shows, by its form, whether it refers to the person or thing spoken to, or to the person or thing spoken of. They are I, we, you, he, she, it, they.
Phrase:	A phrase is a group of related words, without a subject and a predicate (or a finite verb), but which functions as a single part of speech. There are: verb phrase, noun phrase (appositive phrase), prepositional phrase, infinitive phrase, participal phrase and the gerund phrase. The last three are generally referred to as verbal phrases.
Positive Degree:	The positive degree is the simple form of the adjective or adverb which does not, however, indicate any degree of comparison.
Possessive Case:	The possessive case (also called genitive case) is used to mark ownership or possession. Generally, nouns have special forms to show the possessive case and this is done by adding the inflectional suffix "-

	s" separated by an apostrophe to the base of the noun.
Predicate:	The predicate is that part of the sentence that makes a statement about the subject. It consists of the verb alone or some structure in which the verb is more prominent.
Predicate Adjective:	A predicate adjective is an adjective that completes the verb and modifies the subject. A predicate adjective is found in the predicate word. It may be a single word, a phrase or a clause. It can also serve as an adjective or an adverb.
Predicate Noun:	A predicate noun is a noun used after the linking verb. In other words, the predicate noun serves as a complement of the subject joined together by linking verb. It is also called predicate nominative.
Preposition:	A preposition is a word that shows the relationship between its object and some other word in the sentence. It is a function word mainly used together with another word (mostly nouns and pronouns) in the sentence to form a phrase.
Prepositional phrase:	A prepositional phrase is a group of words (usually without a finite verb) which consists of a preposition and its objects but functions as another part
Present Perfect Tense:	The present tense denotes action that is completed at the time of speaking or writing.
Present Tense:	The present tense is the tense form used to denote event or action that occur simultaneously with the moment of

speaking or utterance, or at the present time. Relatively, the present tense may be used to express habitual action, and to mark an idea which is generally accepted as true.

Pronoun: A pronoun is a word used in place of, or to replace, a noun. Some pronouns serve as the subject of the sentence (e.g. I, we, it, she, he, you, they) while others serve as the object) of verb (eg.me,us,it,him,her,you,them).

Verb: A verb is a part of speech which expresses action or state of being which the subject of the sentence performs (in the case of action or relates(in the case of state of being) Verbs exhibit certain characteristics to relate its functions. These include tense, voice, mood and aspect.Verbs are of two types namely principal verb and auxiliary verb which also acts as linking or copulative verb.

Verbal: A verbal is a verb form that is used as another part of speech. Verbal includes participle, gerund and infinitive.

Verb Phrase: A verb phrase is a verb that consists of more than one word. It is composed of a principal verb and one or more auxiliary verbs. It can also be referred to as verbal group when it combines moderators/operators and modal auxiliary verbs. The verbs phrase can equally be composed of the principal verb plus one or more preposition(s).

Voice:	Voice is that property of a verb which shows whether the subject is performing the action or is receiving the action of the verb. Voice is also a technical term which indicates whether the subject is performing the action or is receiving the act of the verb.
Word:	A word is a linguistic term covering any morphological form considered to be independent in distribution nd meaning, and capable of being written with space on either side. Structurally, it may be constituted of one or more morphemes; and the constituent morpheme(s) may be bound or free.

References

Aliu, J. S. (2006). *Upgrading English achievement.* Zaria: Tamaza Publishing Company.

Achebe, Chinua (1996). *A man of the people.* London. Heinemann Educational Books.

Armah, Ayi Kwei (1968). *The beautiful ones are not yet born.* London: Heinemann Educational Books.

Banjo, A. (1996). *Making a virtue of necessity. An overview of the English language in Nigeria.* Ibadan: Ibadan University Press.

Baugh, Albert C. (1976). *A history of English language.* London: Routledge & Kegan Paul.

Bloomfield, L. (1939). *Menomini morphophonemics.* In: Makkal, V.B. (1972). *Phonological theory: evolution and current practice.* New York: Holt, Rineheart & Winston. Pp. 53-64.

Brann, C. M. B. (2006). *Language in education and society: An anthology of selected writings of C. M. B. Brann (1975-2005).* Maiduguri: Faculty of Arts Occassional Publication (FAOP).

Brook, G. L. (1958). *A history of English language,* London: Andre Deutsche.

Cameron, D. (1990). (ed.). "Introduction." In *The feminist critique of language.* London: Routlegde & Kegan Paul. Pp. 1-30.

Chomsky, N. (1968). *Language and mind.* New York: Harcourt Brace.

Crystal, D. (1987). *The Cambridge encyclopedia of language.* New York: Cambridge University Press.

Dinneen, F.P. (1966). *An introduction to general linguistics.* London: Holt, Rinehart and Wiston.

Eka, D. (1985). *Phonological study of standard Nigerian English.* Unpublished Ph.D Dissertation, Ahmadu Bello University (ABU), Zaria.

Eka, D. (1994). *Elements of grammar and mechanics of the English language.* Uyo: Samuf Nigeria.

Eka, D. (2000). *Issues in Nigerian English Usage.* Uyo, Scholar Press (Nig.) Ltd.

Eka, D. & Udofot, I. (1996). *Aspects of spoken language.* Calabar: Bon Universal.

Essien, O. E. (1990). *A grammar of the Ibibio language.* Ibadan: University Press.

Essien, O. E. (2006). Language and the Nigerian reforms agenda. In Ndimele, O., Ikechukwu, C. I. & Mbah, B. M. (eds.). *Language and economic reforms in Nigeria.* Port Harcourt: M & J Grand Orbit Communications.

Francis, W.N (1967). *The English language (an introduction).* London: English University Press.

Fries, C. C. (1952). *Teaching and learning English as a foreign language.* Ann Arbor: University of Michigan Press.

Gleason, H. A.(1961). *An introduction to descriptive Linguistics.* Revised Edition. U.S.A: Holt, Rinehart and Winston.

Gowers, E. (1948). *The complete plain words.* England: Penguin.

Jakobson, R., & Halle, M. (1956). *Fundamentals of language.* The Hague: Mouton.

Jones, E. D. (1960). Sierra Leone and the English language. In: *West African journal of education.* Pp. 10-18.

Josiah, U.E. (1997). Vocabulary development. In Tonga, A.N. (ed.). *Use of English for polytechnics.* Vol. 1. Ibadan: Stiriling- Holder Publishers.

Josiah, U.E. (2002). *Patterns of inflection in English and Ibibio: A contrastive study.* An Unpublished M.A Thesis, University of Uyo, Uyo.

Jowitt, D. (1991). *Nigerian English usage: An introduction.* Lagos: Longman Group.

Kermode, Frank et al. (1973). *Oxford anthology of English literature. Vol. 1.* New York: Oxford University Press.

Ladefoged, P. (1975). *A course in linguistics.* New York: Harcourt Brace Jovanovich.
Lamberts, J.J. (1972). *Fundamentals of linguistic analysis.* New York: Harcourt Brace Jovanovich.
Lyons, J. (1969). *Introduction to theoretical Linguistics.* London: Cambridge University Press.
Crimmon, J.M. et al. (1972). *Writing with a purpose.* Boston: Houghton Mifflin Company.
Mathews, P.H. (1974). *Morphology: An introduction to the theory of word structure.* Cambridge: Cambridge University Press.
McArthur, T. (ed.) (1996). *The Oxford companion of the English language.* Oxford: Oxford University Press.
Muir, J. (1972). *Modern approach to English grammar: An introduction to systemic grammar.* London: B.T. Batsford.
Napoli, J. N. (1996). *Linguistics: An introduction.* Oxford: Oxford University Press.
Oluikpe, Benson O. A. (1981). *The use of English for higher education.* Onitsha: Africana-Feb Publishers.
Osisanwo, W. (2008). Learning modes and appropriate technologies for language learning. A Keynote Address Presented at the 6th National Conference of the National Association of Teachers and Researchers of English as a Second Language (NATRESL), Federal University of Technology, Akure.
Pink, M.A. and Thomas, S.E. (1970). *English grammar: Composition and correspondence.* London: Cassel and Company.
Quirk, R., Greenbaum, S. & Svartvik, J. (1979). *A university grammar of English.* London: Longman Group.
Sapir, E. (1921). *Language: An introduction to the study of speech.* New York: Harcourt Brace Jovanovich.
Spencer, J. (ed.). (1991). *The English language in West Africa.* London: Longman Group.

Tomori. S.H.O. (1977). *The morphology and syntax of present-day English: An introduction.* London: Heinemann Educational Books.

Tonga, A. N. (ed.) (2003). *Use of English for polytechnics.* Vol. 1. 2nd Edition. Bida: Jube Evans.

Udo, I.I.L. (2003). *An introduction to phonemic analysis.* Lagos: Concept Publications.

Udoudom, J. C. (1997). *English and Ibibio morphological systems: A contrastive study.* An Unpublished M.A. Thesis, University of Uyo, Uyo.

Yule, G. (1996). *The study of language.* Second Edition. Cambridge: Cambridge University Press.

www.ingramcontent.com/pod-product-compliance
Lightning Source LLC
Chambersburg PA
CBHW060149050426
42446CB00013B/2736